UNDEFEATED

A PERSONAL GUIDE FOR
SUCCESSFUL LIVING

BY CARLOS JONES II

Printed in the United States of America

ISBN 978-1-7346100-1-7

Sunshine Reigns Publishing Company
(A subsidiary of The Master Communicator's Writing Services)

www.mcwritingservices.com

TABLE OF CONTENTS

DEDICATION

I would like to dedicate this book to the next generation – mainly my children, Summer, Carlos, and Carson. I hope that as they go through life, they will realize that they are undefeated in everything that they do. My prayer is for them to take this information and run with it so that it will lead them to grow leaps and bounds above whatever circumstances they may find themselves in. And as we lead the current generation, I pray that they will be leaders of their time.

And so, I am excited to see what future generations accomplish as they serve the God of all generations.

ACKNOWLEDGEMENTS

First and foremost, I would like to acknowledge God who has given me the inspiration, ability, wisdom, and knowledge to delve into these topics and uncover His truths.

Also, I would like to thank Inspiration Church for giving me the platform to study and deliver these messages. Inspiration Church's media team: Jay, Sivan, Adrian, Randall, Ebony, Kenny, Cynthia, Shamia, Suvon, and Latasia Williamson, and anyone else who's ever served on it, thank you for recording these messages so that I can go back and transcribe them. What you do as a team ensures that each message outlives Sunday.

Words faintly express the love and gratitude I have for my family, but here they are. I am so very thankful to and for my wife who supports me and graciously gives me the time and space to continue God's work. She is often the sounding board for many of my thoughts and ideas. I'm grateful for my children because they show me why these types of books are needed for the next generation.

I thank my parents who continue to support me in ministry and in everything that I do. To my siblings, Carla, Tamara, and Chris Adams: thank you for allowing me to learn from you and speak into your lives about what it means to be undefeated.

A very special thank you to my pastor, Smokie Norful, who continually exposes me to different things that generate creativity. Thanks to my Turo host community. Because of them, I can use and see the methods of this book in real time. They allow me the privilege of watching them grow financially and expand to others who are part of the Inspiration Partners Network.

My thought partners in this writing process assisted with making this book what it is. Thanks to Monique whose invaluable guidance assisted me with organizing my thoughts in a way specifically for my intended audience. Sharon and her team's time and efforts helped this product come to fruition. To Ray, Lance, Brandon Stewart, Daphne, Chris Delaney, Marrick and Muriel, Toure, and many others whom I talk to about what it means to be undefeated – thank you all.

I am thankful for my village at large; this includes everybody I encounter. To all those who support me, whether it be socially, mentally, financially, emotionally, or any other way, I'm thankful that you inspired me to create this work for God's kingdom. I am also grateful for my colleges, Tennessee State and Emory University, that deposited many truths into me. I learned many elements spoken of in this book as a young man through the football department at Tennessee State and Hightower High School. So, I'm grateful for those experiences as well.

Thank you so much for reading this book. I pray that it touches you. Furthermore, I pray that you bless others with this information, so they, too, can live every day undefeated.

FOREWORD

When I first was asked to write the foreword to this book, I was honored. A key catalyst for me to make this written contribution came when I turned to the page where Pastor Carlos Jones II quotes one of my favorite authors and leaders, Dr. Myles Munroe. Dr. Munroe said, "Don't die old; die empty." At that point, I said "yes." Then, as I read it, I emphatically said "yes" and could not stop reading this wonderful, inspirational, and transformational book.

This book could not have come at a better time. Wars, rumors of wars, the pandemic, outrage from years of social injustice, and so many other emotions are being evoked as a result of these and other activities in what we may refer to as perilous times. Pastor Jones, pens this book when the world and those in it are greatly scurrying to redeem the time that has been "lost." Many are wandering aimlessly, numbed by society. Many are feeling defeated as though they have not accomplished much or feel as though they have failed. This book is a must-read!

The book, *Undefeated*, challenges the reader to get out of the quagmire caused by external environments and self-imposed thoughts. Through effective story-telling and spiritual references, Pastor Jones weaves a winning combination to catapult the reader from sitting on the sidelines (couch) to "jumping in the game of life." When life hits as hard as it has for us, there is a recalibration needed. For some, it is a tweak, a word of encouragement, but for others, it is a major shift to new habits by empowering the mind through definitive affirmations and prayer.

Undefeated encourages you to do whatever it takes to be victorious on the field, in business, ministry, family, relationships, or other arenas. Your negative past experiences can be revolutionized to bring about a new you full of life and hope. As a man (or woman) thinks in his (or her heart) so is he or she.

We must make a point to focus on the good. Pastor Jones encourages us to not have a self-fulfilling prophecy with words of defeat. Take away the negative self-talk and put ourselves in an environment with those whom we want to be around. This strategy reinforces what the Bible says, *"Finally, brethren, whatsoever things are true, whatsoever things are honest, whatsoever things are just, whatsoever things are pure, whatsoever things are lovely, whatsoever things are of good report; if there be any virtue, and if there be any praise, think on these things"* (Philippians 4:8 KJV).

Do not let peer pressure get to you. Stay focused. Let positive affirmations and the directions given to you by the Holy Spirit lead you. If you do not have a clue how to transform your thinking, this book will do that. If you are saying to yourself, "I do not have anyone in my circle of friends and family who surrounds me with positive words and gestures of love," then look no further. This book will indeed be a guidepost and refreshing breath of life inspired by God that will resuscitate you, the reader, with new beliefs.

Continue to do what Pastor Jones says and do not give up hope. *"Be not weary in well doing, for in due season you will reap if you faint not"* (Galatians 6:9 KJV). Happy reading as you launch forward to being Undefeated.

Marina Angelica Coryat, Author
The Due [Dü] Season

INTRODUCTION

One of the most miraculous realities of our humanity is that everyone has been predestined to live an undefeated life by master design. Over the centuries mankind has become more proficient in mastering resilience and understanding this truth. The evidence is even more apparent in the millennials and those who have come before us. I say "us" because I proudly live this life as a millennial.

You may be wondering, *Who Am I?* That's a good question! I'm glad you asked.

I am a born leader who lives his life to inspire others. Since my childhood, I have used my voice and my truth to captivate audiences. I gained national attention on *America's Funniest Home Videos* as the five-year-old boy who literally screamed his ABCs while at a school program. Little did I know, my young, developing voice was already at work. I went on to complete my primary and secondary education and later attended college with my sights set on earning a position with the National Football League. I graduated college;

however, my aspirations of becoming a pro athlete were cut short when God gave me a new direction for my life.

Leaving my football aspirations behind, at the leading of God, I acknowledged the ministry calling on my life. I hold a Bachelor of Arts degree in Psychology and a Master's in Divinity which I received at Candler School of Theology at Emory University in Atlanta, GA. During my tenure, at Tennessee State, I served as the President of the Fellowship of Christian Athletes which allowed me to start a new path as a servant leader to my teammates.

After returning home, I started The Way Interdenominational Church and led a congregation there for seven years. In 2017 I partnered with Pastor Smokie Norful to launch Inspiration Church where I lead a multi-generational body of believers. I currently provide greater Houston's Pearland and Missouri City communities with an inspiring message of hope, healing, and empowerment. Admittedly, I have worked to accomplish quite a bit in my life but not without mistakes, delays, and difficulties. I am sure you can relate to this.

Similar to previous generations, we have faced tragedy and trials and risen above their circumstances, even to the point of creating new solutions. We have been plagued with a worldwide pandemic, economic instability, rising housing and gas costs, a corrupt political system, unprecedented climate change, food and financial insecurity, gun violence like no other time in history, mental health concerns, and a host of other challenges. But, in the words of the famous poet laureate, Maya Angelou, … "still [we] rise!" If you are looking for something to define the word "undefeated," just stick a picture of a group of millennials on the page.

The word undefeated is often defined as the ability to win consecutive battles or contests where two opposing forces attempt to outperform each other in a precarious situation. Here's the breakdown of the word as I see it: "Un" meaning to do the opposite of what's expected. "Defeated" meaning to lose a war or a battle. On the battlefield of life, one of the most intense conflicts is the one between good and evil. We already know how this will end. But until the final outcome, God instructs us to defeat evil with good (Romans 12:21).

Not every challenge we encounter is a result of evil. Some challenges are simply tests and trials we must go through to get stronger and become more of what God wants us to be. Whether we face divinely designed challenges or those associated with evil, we can do so with positive thinking, a level of assurance, and unwavering confidence that we will triumph over any threat or negative situation. Living undefeated does not keep us from obstacles; it equips us with the God-given mentality to successfully and confidently navigate those obstacles.

Every undefeated champion remembers what it took to win. You might wonder how someone prepares to wear the title. The right preparation often begins with perspective. The champion-to-be sees hardships in life as an opportunity to prepare for greater things and bigger accomplishments to come. The late Chadwick Boseman had this to say about the preparation stage: "Sometimes you need to feel the pain and sting of defeat to activate the real passion and purpose that God predestined inside of you."[1]

The very genesis of this book is based on the premise that we all have an undefeated champion inside of us. That does not mean that you won't face tests, trials, disappointments, or even setbacks. It does not mean that you won't be on many battlefields in life, but it does mean that you will ultimately win the war.

This book will provide you with champion-level preparation to help you accomplish the goal of living an undefeated life. It includes guidelines I use for approaching challenges as more than

---

[1] Foust, Michael. Chadwick Boseman was a Christian who quoted Scripture, told students "God predestined" their future. 31 Aug. 2020, https://www.christianheadlines.com.

the "conqueror" the Word of God proclaims me to be (Romans 8:37). I live undefeated, and you can too.

Here are four principles I use to live an undefeated life that I will address in this book:

1. *No One Is Assigned a Life of Defeat*: Absolutely no one has been placed on this earth or born into this world with the assignment to be defeated. Say this with me... *I am not assigned to a defeated life.*

2. *Defeat Is Not a Pathway to Purpose for Anyone*: Regardless of race, religion, age, gender, environment, sex, creed, belief system, handicap, normalcy, exceptionality, economic status, or education – no matter who you are, your assignment or purpose is not to live defeated. So, if you are on a pathway riddled with defeat, you are not on a purpose-driven pathway.

3. *Living an Undefeated Lifestyle Is Living a Well-Satisfied Life*: Ask yourself the following questions: Are you living a well-satisfied life? Look around. What do you see? A well-satisfied life is cultivated by your belief system, your deep knowing or faith in God and self, and knowing how and why you were designed for what purpose. Don't measure your intrinsic or extrinsic wealth by the things you possess, because there are people in the world with everything. God gave Adam and Eve everything in the Garden of Eden, but they lacked obedience and self-control, which caused their defeat.

4. *All Power Has Been Given to You!* You're in control of your decisions. You may ask the question, "What about people born with inabilities?" Don't give yourself the right to establish your inabilities as your norm. Have you placed yourself in a personal prison? Our decisions are our choice – whatever mark we want to make in life, we can do so. I expanded on this concept in a previous series of sermons, "Pursuit of Purpose" (P.O.P.)[2] God has given you the grace and peace of mind to complete any task that He has assigned you to do. You are hard-wired with everything that you need to live an undefeated life.

Our Main Power Source, God

I often get my inspiration to live an undefeated life from the Bible. Numerous stories in the book of books give us biblical proof that we are true champions, and we have the power to live an undefeated life when we add God to the equation. As a boy, these stories fueled my ability to accomplish my goals. My father is a preacher, so I had lots of opportunities to hear Bible stories. I had the pleasure of growing up in church. My family and I attended Community Fellowship Baptist Church of Missouri City, Texas (on the outskirts of Houston), where my father was the pastor. I am technically a third-generation pastor, as my great grandfather on my mother's side was also a pastor. You might say it was destined for me as well.

---

[2] P.O.P. You are gifted Pastor Carlos Jones Sr. YouTube. 17 Jan. 2021, https://www.youtube.com/watch?app=desktop&v=D-E9GY7-q1s.

One story that inspires me is that of David and Goliath. David was a scrawny good looking young man that made the heart of women melt. When the Prophet Samuel came to the house of Jesse looking for a king, he didn't even bother to bring David to the forefront. David just didn't fit the profile. The prophet examined all of Jesse's sons and said, "None of these are the next King of Israel. Is there anyone else?" Jesse sent someone to the shepherd's field to get David. Instantly when he was placed in the lineup of potential kings, Samuel said, "He's the one." Everyone had counted David out, but God. Everyone may count you out, but they don't have a clue of the greatness that has been invested in you by your Creator.

That same David was sent to the battlefield by his father with food for his brothers when Israel and the Philistines were at war. David's brother tried to make a spectacle of him in front of his fellow soldiers. David ignored him and went about his business. He just happened to show up when Goliath, a giant nearly ten feet tall covered in bronze armor from head to toe made an appearance. Goliath insulted the Israeli army with threats and challenges and even cursed their God. Previously, the Israeli army would simply run away in fear when he showed up, but Goliath caught David's attention. David accepted the challenge and gathered the courage to fight this giant of a man.

The king of Israel at that time offered his armor, but David refused it because he hadn't proved it. In other words, he did not have proof of its success through personal experience. He decided instead to use the tools he was familiar with, five smooth stones and a slingshot. See David had used these tools before to slay a lion and a bear, so he was confident of their ability to perform for him. When facing the giant, he found strength in the fact that he was not alone in this battle. God, Himself, was fighting with David! God had predestined David to win this battle. Some may say that the fight was fixed! It took one stone to kill Goliath strategically placed in the center of his forehead. He fell over, face first, and the Philistine army ran like a bunch of scared pigs.

The moral of this story is that we all possess the power to kill the giants we face in life. It may appear that we are outnumbered, outmaneuvered, weak, and powerless, but there is a greater force inside of us that causes us to win. We must intentionally tap into that main power source when we face the giants in our lives. Remember the fight is fixed, and you win!

You have it in you, even when it doesn't look like it. This book was written with the specific purpose of empowering you to cultivate an undefeated mentality and to live your life accordingly. It's obvious in the world that we live in it's a necessary tool to live a maximized existence. My prayer is that you will take the principles

I share in this book and not only equip yourself to prosper for such a time as this but to help others also flourish.

Developing an Undefeated Mindset

Popularity early in my life thrust my family and me into the national spotlight. Because of my performance, my family became the first African Americans to win *America's Funniest Home Video's* grand prize. We became instant celebrities. I remember vividly how quickly things started to change; I recall being in Jet magazine and appearing on several Today shows. It was exhilarating. I was far too young to be affected by the stress of it all. One thing I did learn was the sweet taste of instant success from this experience. As a child, this experience did wonders for my self-esteem and began the formation of a champion mindset. It carried me throughout my early academic experience until high school when I came face-to-face with what I thought at the time was a major negative influence.

During my tenure in high school, I was in Spring Training to prepare for the upcoming school year. My previous team had a reputation for being the best in the state, so I'd already experienced an unusual level of success. Imagine my surprise when my new coach started treating me like I was a rookie. I couldn't do anything right, and he let the entire world know it in language that I wouldn't want my mother to hear. He considered my performance substandard. I wasn't used to this kind of treatment. I knew I had skills, but for some reason, this particular coach couldn't see it, so I quit the team. When I got to his office, I turned in my jersey and left him there to contemplate my surprise decision.

Several days later, he showed up at one of my classes and pulled me to the side to talk with me. I gave him a tough time because I wasn't on the team anymore. I didn't think I had to listen to anything he had to say. To my surprise, he explained that he'd been hard on me because he saw my exceptional potential. If I was going to lead the team to a victorious season, I needed more training and grooming to get to that level of competence. Same game, similar rules, but I was required to perform at a higher level of proficiency to see his prophecy become a reality. Once I understood the method for his madness, I could make the necessary personal adjustments. It still wasn't comfortable, but a change was necessary for me to have an undefeated season. It benefited me personally and the team.

That high school experience further shaped my champion mindset. I did whatever it took to be undefeated on and off the football field. I became receptive to strategies the coach shared. My work ethic shifted. My drive to be the best intensified. I worked at a higher level to attain my athletic goals, and it paid off. When I graduated high school, I was accepted into Tennessee State University, Nashville on a full athletic scholarship. My fierce work ethic put me in a position to participate in the NFL Combine. The Combine was one step closer to my ultimate goal of being a professional football player.

Of course, God had a different plan for my life. However, none of my experiences were wasted. Motivation to walk with godly confidence followed me when I answered God's call to work in purpose and on purpose. My purposed path was not without roadblocks. But God faithfully acted as my navigation. He patiently molded my mind. As my teacher, God educated me on how to connect with individuals who needed practical explanations of the Gospel. As my guide, He whispered truths that provided direction as I traveled many states to preach the Word. Being obedient to this calling required dedication, tenacity, and the ability to strategize like I learned to do as an athlete.

Here are the four key strategies that helped me develop an undefeated mindset:

1. Memorize Scripture (or Positive Affirmations) – Memorizing God's word (or memorizing positive affirmations) and applying it to your life lays the foundation for genuine victory on the battlefield of life. Throughout this book, I will show you how to effectively address the struggles and trials that you may face in life by changing your thought process from negative to positive like an undefeated champion.

2. Chase Down Negative Thoughts – You are the gatekeeper of your mind. You can and will be able to take charge of your thoughts and anything that doesn't line up with your destiny after reading this book.

3. Selectively Open Doors – An open door is an invitation for anyone to come in. You must be more specific about what you want to walk through the doors that lead to your heart and mind. You also have to be diligent in guarding that door to keep all the enemies (negative thoughts, unexpected trials, disappointments, broken dreams) to your purpose from entering. I will specifically lay out a step-by-step procedure in this book to assist you in accomplishing this goal.

4. Speak the Language of the Undefeated – Negative words bring about negative results. Positive words bring positive results and lead to a life of victory. In this book, I will teach you how to access an undefeated lifestyle, simply by changing the way you talk about yourself and your lifestyle.

These strategies are instrumental in my work for the ministry and my daily walk.

Unbound: Pressing Toward Purpose

Some people may have unique circumstances that could hinder

them from attaining personal goals or working within their purpose. Those challenges might be mental, physical, or emotional and could very well bind individuals, further hindering their purposed path.

Unfortunately, some people living for God have a poverty mentality. They don't think they deserve the life that God has promised them. Those individuals are bound by depraved thinking. But God is a covenant keeper! He has promised to never break His covenant with His creation. You are undefeated because God predestined you for success. God reminds us of His commitment to the sun and moon and equates His dedication to us with that unbreakable covenant (Jeremiah 33:14-26). In other words, His promise will be yours as long as the sun and the moon exist. That sounds like forever to me.

Physical or cognitive disabilities also pose challenges unique to individuals that the general population doesn't have to worry about. Depending on their mindset, those with disabilities could be confined within certain limits. However, having a physical or cognitive disability is not an excuse. There are numerous champions with disabilities who made a mark on the world like Amanda Gorman, Harriet Tubman, Wilma Rudolph, Halle Berry, Daymond John, and Stevie Wonder to name a few.

Being physically locked up is another example of confinement that doesn't have to dictate a person's outcome. Some people may consider being bound in prison as a game-changer in life. If anything could possibly derail your purpose, this could. But that wasn't the case for Robert Downey Jr., Tim Allen, Christian Slater, Charles Colson, and Martha Stewart. They latched on to their pursuit of purpose and used that experience to solidify their commitment to living an undefeated life – one unbound to any restraint – despite once being physically locked up.

As humans, we are flawed and subject to making the wrong decisions that sometimes bring about negative consequences. Those consequences might appear in the form of obstacles. We should think about why we are in that situation and what we can do to bring about desired results. But we shouldn't worry. Whether you encounter difficulties because of decisions you made or things out of your control, God will never fail. Even when we fail ourselves through unfavorable choices, God remains faithful. Our responsibility lies in choosing to get and remain on a purposed path.

Whatever mark you want to make in life, you can do it. God has given you the grace and peace of mind to do so. You are hardwired by the "Master Electrician" with everything you need to be a champion. Not just with the tools to build a constructive pathway to fulfill your destiny, but also the ability to overcome any obstacles that may come your way. Apostle Paul was a prime example of being an undefeated champion. He wrote over half of the New Testament while in prison.

The individuals I mentioned didn't like the direction their paths were headed, so they decided to change their storyline. If you don't like where your story is going, you can change it. You've been given the power; what you do with it is determined by you. You make decisions that propel you forward in life. I am not specifically talking about having a successful career or mastering your job skills. Rather, I speak of living life to the fullest in the abundance God has promised. I am talking about pressing toward purpose, living the life that God has given you, and doing so without a limited mindset.

Undefeated: Strategizing for a Life of Purpose

Undefeated, the book, is a power manual designed to help you navigate life. I use the word "power" because you have to possess a certain level of it to live an unbeatable life. I recognized the power of submitting to authority. It was my choice to step up my game so that I could be an asset to the team and fulfill my coach's expectations. He saw things in me that were undeveloped and raw. Why? Because he had the experience and ability to recognize talent after coaching hundreds of high school students to win.

On a sovereign level, my Creator crafted and equipped me to fulfill my calling. He activated all that was placed in me to carry out His divine purpose. Part of that was my developing strategies to become the best athlete possible when winning wasn't enough. Another part was my surrendering to the counsel of the Holy Spirit who effectively guided me through each task set before me. I chose to be equipped to win in athletics and ministry. You will have to do likewise if you are going to live an undefeated life.

I happen to be writing this book in one of the most diverse cities in the United States. It is the fourth largest city in our country where many undefeated champions reside. I will share their stories throughout this book because contrary to popular opinion, an everyday person can live an undefeated life with God's help. As you move through the pages of this book, it is my goal to get you fired up to live undefeated and take action. When you've got the power, potential, and positive attitude necessary to live a life of abundance, the sky's the limit.

CHAPTER ONE
A Life Undefeated

Just because a person lives a life undefeated does not mean that individual has not encountered difficult times. Some people do not look like what they have been through. The one person that you might think has always had everything together could have gone through a tragic experience. Would you believe that situations or circumstances just might have destroyed that individual's goals, and opportunities, and even put a damper on his or her spirit? Destruction has such a negative connotation; however, fortune and redemption have come from destruction.

Destroyed but Not Defeated

Destruction in life can strike at any time. Typically, it happens to us when we least expect it. Take my situation with my high school coach, for example. I had played with top-tier football talent in the state of Texas. I was recognized as the best among the best.

I approached Spring Training with a high level of confidence. Imagine my surprise and dismay when the coach's feedback didn't match what I was used to receiving. I completed drills and ran familiar plays. In my mind, I was putting forth my best effort and would receive compliments from the coach. I received the direct opposite. It felt like the coach gave me corrective feedback after every single play. I listened, adjusted, and continuously ran subsequent plays exerting all the athletic skills and abilities I had. Despite my best efforts, I was consistently told my performance was not meeting the mark.

Similar to Kobe Bryant's first few years in the NBA, my first couple of weeks of Spring Training were a low point in my high school football career. I went through a level of frustration far beyond anything I had ever experienced. I knew my abilities, yet the coach continuously pointed out faults, and he did so with demeaning words. I viewed the coach as unfair, and I thought there was nothing I could do on the football field to gain his approval. My self-esteem was briefly destroyed, but like Kobe Bryant, I was nowhere close to being defeated.

Sometimes we must be broken down to be rebuilt to our purpose. I later learned to appreciate the experience and allow it to make me better instead of bitter. It wasn't until I was able to clearly understand God's intent with a much more mature mind that I was able to make an undefeated life a part of my expectancy. I recognized that to live undefeated, I could not allow things from my past to control my ability to maximize my future potential.

I am sure my football experience pales in comparison to countless stories of others who also live undefeated lives, one being Dante Bowe. He is an undefeated champion.

His song "Champion" (recorded in 2019 by Bethel Music) constantly reminds me that it is no one's destined to be defeated. He is the main artist featured on the album, *Revival's in the Air*. Bowe was raised by a mother and father who sold drugs so that he and his siblings could have a better life. This may make you wonder where the church's influence comes from. He had a grandfather who was a preacher and a grandmother who loved Jesus. They exposed him to the church, and he fell in love with the idea of having a relationship with the Savior who offered unconditional love.

Bowe's parents supported him, but he still experienced hardships in life. At a young age, he was molested. As an adult, he found himself homeless and living on the streets. Statistics say that he was headed for a life of panhandling on street corners and early death, but God had other plans for him.

Today, he certainly does not look like what he went through. He is now one of the most sought-after Christian artists in the nation. His music has a way of shouting hope and redemption. He does not sing out of his experience; he sings in a manner of unconditional praise and continual chorus. Co-writing the single "Champion" is a true expression of his appreciation and understanding that God is the cause of his success in living an undefeated life.

In an article featured in *Jubilee Cast*, Bowe had this to say about the story behind the song:

> The inspiration for "Champion" came from a conversation with friends about identity, what the Father has done for us, and our awareness of that. This song is personal, not just for me, but for anyone who's ever felt the pressure to measure up or has felt lesser than. We all, at some point in our lives, walk through a season of insecurity and doubt in what the Lord has already spoken. Even when we know what He says, it seems unfair for a good God to still esteem and give power to those who were once sinners. Once we understand His Lordship and Kingship, we realize just how powerful we are as joint heirs with Christ. We didn't work for it. We didn't earn it. It's just simply our inheritance. Once we learn that, everything changes.[3]

We are the agents of change positioned by God in our assigned geographical spaces. Sometimes we are forced to run into that reality like we would a brick wall – unexpectedly and with trepidation. Nevertheless, we are not assigned a life of defeat. Living a life of purpose sometimes means navigating obstacles that momentarily hinder our physical and mental fortitude and test our resolve. That is exactly what happened with Bowe and me. No matter what, we continued walking our individual paths as undefeated individuals. We boldly stand on our platforms for Christ because we already know that the end will be victory through Christ Jesus! You are a part of that victorious ending.

Say it with us: "We are not assigned to a life of defeat!"

However, destruction sometimes happens to the land around us, our communities, and the people we know. Mass destruction of any type seems hopeless. But the God we serve has a way of

[3] Jubilee Cast. Bethel Music 'Revival's in the Air' album review. Jubilee Cast, 28 May 2020, https://www.jubileecast.com.

bringing about fortune and restoration from reprobate people and obliterated places.

Fortune from Destruction

Dynamite is deadly. It destroys. The right amount of it collapses buildings, wipes out cities, and decimates nations. Although each of those statements is true about dynamite, they present a one-sided view of it.

When Alfred Bernhard Nobel first created dynamite, he recognized its ability to destroy nations and people, and protect groups of people who otherwise would be consumed by the greed of larger nations. The prominent defense mechanism, preservation, was Nobel's original intent. Dynamite is good when it's used to preserve a nation by increasing its ability to defend the people and land.

Everyone didn't see dynamite the same way Nobel did. What Nobel envisioned as a tool to help and preserve, others saw as an opportunity to demolish and destroy. It's strange how what one individual creates for good, another one perverts it to something bad. How familiar does that sound? Satan has been twisting the goodness of God and the righteous efforts of his people since the beginning. But we know *"all things work together for those who are called according to His purpose"* (Romans 8:28 MEV).

Now, I am not saying that Nobel was a Christian. I do not have any information to confirm whether he was or not. However, history proves he had good intentions. One of the things we can learn from Nobel is that we will have struggles, even if we are trying to do what is right. Nobel created dynamite but couldn't control how it would be used once it was in other people's hands. I can only imagine the burden Nobel felt knowing his invention was used to dismantle people's lives when his intent was just the opposite. To say he must have been deeply disturbed by the violence of his invention would probably be an understatement.

The perversion of his invention did not set well with Nobel, so he didn't rest. He became concerned with establishing worldwide peace. He did not want to leave a legacy of death and destruction.

Its multipurpose use made dynamite a popular product. Nobel became wealthy by setting up companies and selling patent rights to dynamite and related commodities worldwide. He made large profits to the point that he left a sizable estate as an endowment for annual Nobel Prize awards when he died.

Nobel made a fortune from his invention which had the power to destroy. He turned that wealth into something that would continuously celebrate the good that men do here on earth. He intentionally turned a defeatist situation into something that instead brings good results because he had an undefeated mindset. As a result, he found a way to bless others from what some used as a destructive force.

Restoration from Destruction
Destruction isn't always bad. In fact, destruction can be used as an act of defense and restoration. Some things need to be eradicated because of their potential to destroy all of mankind. When we look at the story of Noah, we see that God destroyed the earth because of man's wickedness (Genesis 6-9).

The wonderful thing about the God we serve is He gives us a choice in everything. We can choose right or wrong, good or bad, positive or negative, to help or to hurt, and to follow God's plan or not to follow it. During Noah's time, most people chose to do things outside of God's will. They acted selfishly and with impure motives. God was not pleased. The people's decisions and actions grieved God to the point that He was "sorry" that He made man (Genesis 6:6 CSB).

I was once told that the safest place is always in the will of God. This was true for Noah and subsequently his family. While a majority of the people engaged in what they wanted to do and how they wanted to do it, Noah's ear and aim were poised for God. That is why God entrusted Noah with details of what would happen during the destruction and eventual restoration of the earth. He also told Noah what to do to prepare.

Noah listened and meticulously followed God's instructions, which led Noah to build an ark of safety for him, his family, and some chosen animals. When we listen, God's guidance provides specific instructions. They may not make sense at the time, but God's divine instructions always lead us, his children, to better places far greater than we could ever imagine. Choosing not to listen or follow God's instructions may lead to unnecessary delay or devastation. Noah tried to warn his neighbors of the impending destruction, but they ignored him and went on living their lives as usual.

In God's designated timing the rain started. Noah and his family, along with a male and female version of every animal that existed on earth filled the ark. Everything that was not in the ark was destroyed. Flood waters literally washed away all of mankind! This destruction was necessary because of the decrepit status of mankind. To redeem the earth from utter destruction, God touched the heart of a faithful servant and saved him and his family to preserve the earth. The prominent defense mechanism here was restoration.

The Undefeated Savior

God always had a plan for the redemption of man. We choose whether we walk in the fullness of His plan for our lives. When we make that choice, we are in a constant state of metamorphosis, becoming what God originally intended us to be before Adam's fall in the Garden of Eden. He sent Jesus to seal the deal.

Jesus is the prime example of how suffering can build a bridge to an undefeated lifestyle. Think about how He redeemed all of mankind with a single drop of His blood.

It appeared that Jesus had lost the fight for the freedom of mankind. He was accused, convicted, beaten, and crucified. Satan thought he had won the war. Jesus was dead. God's plan failed, and he had won. At least, that's how Satan perceived it.

Little did Satan know, Jesus' role was to become an offering, a sacrificed lamb without sin. He had to be empty to carry all the sins that would ever exist in the world. Our sins. When He was removed from the cross, and His body placed in a borrowed tomb, it looked hopeless. He was defeated, and everyone who ever took a breath was defeated also. But God… in the midnight hour sent His resurrection power to the Earth, and Jesus rose from the tomb, took the keys to hell and death from the hands of his archenemy, and declared… *I am he that liveth, and was dead, and behold, I am alive forevermore, Amen; and have the keys of hell and of death* (Revelation 1:18 KJV).

Jesus is humanity's superhero. He paid a huge price to prove that living an undefeated life is possible for all of mankind. His life paid the ultimate price, granting us a permanent pardon for our past, present, and future sins. You are undefeated because He is undefeated!

A promise is a declaration of intent to do something in the future or a particular event that will ultimately take place. God gave us over 7,487 promises in the Bible. Jesus also left us promises during his brief ministry here on earth. Some of these include a heavenly mansion, eternal life, forgiveness, supernatural peace, knowing the truth and the freedom associated with it, being our intercessor in

Heaven, love, bearing fruit when we do good works, and rewards. He also to left us a helper, the Holy Spirit.

Often, we may find ourselves in a hard place where defeat causes us to question our future. But that doesn't negate the promises from our Heavenly Father. Danica's story is a great example of God's faithfulness and why our mistakes are not our legacy. She got pregnant at the age of nineteen when a lot of young women are contemplating graduating from college. Considering that the odds were stacked against her as a single mother, alone, some may say she was doomed to live a life of poverty. She said, "Not so!" She embraced the salvation that God offered her and found the courage to locate the undefeated champion. Just as God intended, she aligned herself with His promises. Now, she is an assistant principal and owns a house bigger than mine. It wasn't the career or job that made the difference; it was the saving grace of God and His unconditional love for His child.

When we remember what Jesus did for us on the cross, it puts us in another headspace. He promised to redeem us, and He did. When we accept Him, we get the benefit of His promises; we know that our afflictions are only temporary. Our burdens are not as heavy when we accept God's help with handling them. Jesus taught us that being undefeated requires complete surrender to Him, His plan, and His purpose for your life. The miracle of the cross brought mankind so much more than we could ever imagine. May this book continually serve as a reminder of what it cost God for you to live an undefeated life; His only begotten son was part of that price.

Jesus is the greatest GOAT (Greatest of All Time)! It's an undisputed fact. Usually, people wear this illustrious title when they have performed exceptionally well in their field or profession. It is commonly used as a reference to athletes or musicians. Take a look at some of the people in our generation who wear the same title. Simone Biles, LeBron James, Venus and Serena Williams, Taylor

Swift, Beyonce, Justin Bieber, Mark Zuckerberg, Billie Eilish, are considered champions in their respective industries; however, none of them have died so that all of humanity could live.

With the help of his Father, Jesus conquered the grave. That same resurrection power that abided in Him, abides in you! It's your choice to turn it on or off or to not even acknowledge its presence. In the words of the iconic Isley Brothers, "It's your thing, do what you wanna do." But don't miss out on the greatest gift given to all mankind. I encourage you not to leave this gift unopened.

The truth is that the ability for living an undefeated life abides deep within us all. It is a gift from God that accompanies His desire to bless us beyond our imagination simply because we are His creation. He is a good God, who wants to do good things for His children. The ability to create or be creative is one of those good things we have been blessed with. For example, I am an entrepreneur, and I help create other opportunities for people who seek the same thing. I am also an author, and I create books that help people live out their God-designed purpose with excellence. In other words, I wear a white hat by choice. My service is dedicated to benefiting others. I believe good intentions create good results.

Rising to Power
God has gifted us a superpower of sorts to live the life of a champion. You have complete access to Him and that superpower twenty-four hours a day, seven days a week. Nothing stands in the way of your walking in it, but you. Even Satan cannot stop you from being undefeated! He may be victorious in a few battles, but you get to win the war, as long as you fully understand the mission, accept it, and respond affirmatively. It can't be just having an understanding of what you should do, but you must move beyond your comfort zone and into action. Don't get stuck in your doubts. Imagine superman, never using his superpowers to save the world from utter destruction just because he had a weakness for kryptonite.

We all have weaknesses.

God knew that and made provision for us in Christ Jesus to be His righteousness. Jesus' death on the cross means we are in right standing with God and equipped to be His representatives. We are humans imbued with the God-given power to be champions and conquerors. Move forward with the expectancy of a champion and live the undefeated life that Jesus died for you to have. As He arose from the dead, may you arise in the power He has given you!

The Undefeated Champion's Prayer

Father,
Thank You for Your gifts of love and guidance. Thank you, God, for being the ultimate victor over every battle. Most of all thank You, Father, for being the warring counselor within me who encourages me to stand against the challenges of this life.

You know my struggles. Please set me free from anything that would hinder me from embracing Your truth. Remove everything that stands in the way of me possessing Your promises. You, Father, are greater than anyone or anything in this world, so I know nothing or no one will prosper against Your will for my life. I praise You in advance for Your strength and power to live undefeated.

In Jesus' name, I pray, Amen.

CHAPTER TWO
Defeated by Nature

Sometimes the odds are just stacked against us. Not everyone believes that, but it's true. Unfavorable situations we had nothing to do with produce adverse circumstances out of our control, and we must deal with them the best way we can. As some people say, it is the nature of the beast – one we've been fighting since the beginning.

Deceit Leads to Defeat

Things are not always the way they appear and sound. I can attest to this. There have been times I thought a situation could be better, even when I was living at a level of comfort and blessedness that others could only dream of.

This was also the case for Adam and Eve. They lived in what some describe as a utopia, a perfect world created by God. It was His pleasure to make them happy because He created them for personal fellowship. However, that perfection was challenged the day that the snake had an interesting conversation with Eve. The conversation challenged the way of life that God had commanded Adam and Eve to live by.

Adam was in charge of the garden. He let the snake deceive him into taking a bite of the forbidden fruit through the love of his life (Eve). It was sweet, but it soon became bitter because it cost Adam everything – his home, job, innocence, etc.! For a moment he forgot who he was and why he existed. We all have that momentary lapse of judgment when it's beneficial, which often leads to a defeated mindset and position.

Deceit leads to defeat, and failure ain't pretty. Adam found that out when God called for him in the garden after they ate the forbidden fruit. He was suddenly aware of his limited humanity and the frailty of his human nature. He went from favored son to fallen son. To make matters worse, the consequences of Adam's action affected way more people than him and Eve. It affected everyone born after him. It was the origin of the degradation of all mankind.

The nature of man was forever changed for the worse.

Defeated by Nature

Have you ever wondered where chaos and confusion come from and why there is so much of it? Why do some people make decisions that damage themselves and others around them? I understand why. People constantly fight battles they are unaware of. Those battles originated from the fall. It's the seed of Adam – the nature of man – a defeated nature we all wrestle against. This might sound farfetched, but it is evidenced in history and current experiences.

It didn't take long for Adam and Eve's consequential decision to show up in their children's interactions. The repercussion of their choice deeply embedded itself into the nature of their offspring, and their older son, Cain murdered their younger son, Abel because of envy, jealousy, and sibling rivalry. Those reasons should sound familiar. Competition and animosity remain grave hindrances and disruptions amongst brothers and sisters today.

In the actual Garden of Eden, Eve was tempted to be like God, and Adam didn't want to be left behind. She envied God's authority and secretly yearned to be the Creator of all things. Satan tempted her with the very thing that got him thrown out of Heaven: prominence, position, and power. So yes, it all ties back to the Devil's deceit that corrupted the nature of man, even the innocent among us.

Have you ever wondered why one of the babies' first words is "no"? It's because they are programmed for rebellion. Do you have to teach a toddler how to hit another child or steal a toy? No! Do you have to show them how to tell a lie or get angry when they are forced to share? No! We all have a natural inclination to do the wrong thing. As a direct descendant of Adam, you were born to fail. It wasn't God's intention for your life, but because of Adam's choice, it's something that we all have to live with unless we accept the gift that was sent to straighten out the mess called humanity.

Adam really screwed things up!

You may be thinking, what a brutal assessment of mankind. But go online to your local news and do your own personal evaluation. Then go to the national news and the international news and see if this assessment is valid. What did you find?

Take this a step further. Go into the newspaper archives, 10 years ago, 20 years ago, 100 years ago (this may require a trip to your local library). What did you find? My point is, that even though the odds may seem to be stacked against you, living a defeated, decrepit, sin-filled life wasn't in God's original plan. You might wonder why we are talking about this. To change a lie to the truth, you must pull it up from its roots. So, asking the question of how man got into this mess in the first place is a part of the solution.

Encountering Man's Defeated Nature
The defeated nature of man takes on many forms, especially on the football field. At times it shows when players talk trash to each other. The player who wants to elevate himself or make his skills seem better than another might ridicule an opposing player or even his teammate. Trash talking does one of two things: either it motivates the other player to put forth more effort, or it makes him feel smaller and cave into the pressure. Either way, it arouses the defeated nature in the individual on the receiving end of the taunts and jibes.

Somewhere along the way, high school coaches adopted the philosophy and style of coaching that included humiliating student players. They thought cursing and screaming a bevy of putdowns would make players put forth better efforts. Does that not sound like a defeated nature of man at work or what? Back then, it was a widely accepted practice of football coaching, one I did not understand and strongly resisted.

I remember when my high school coach was using me as his verbal punching bag, how I wrestled with the uncertainty of my football career. I brought my "A" game to the table. I was healthy, young, disciplined, and a proven success. I was a good kid who was being torn down for trying my best. The coach obviously had a problem that certainly wasn't mine. I couldn't figure out his reason for the demeaning behavior. I just knew it didn't feel good. It was messing with my mind.

The defeated nature of man can be encountered in different walks and levels of life. It crops up in the intimate relations between husbands and wives, the everyday interactions of siblings, competition among football players, and even the style of football coaching.

A World Defeated

Think about how the stories I've discussed relate to your personal experiences and what is going on around you. The story of Adam and Eve is truly about lost innocence and the transition that brings self-awareness. One minute everything was perceived to be perfect, but once their eyes were opened, the whole world seemed to be tarnished. This brought self-doubt, lost purpose, and drive. Think about it. All of these are symptoms of depression. Cain and Abel brought hate, violence, destruction, and lust for power. Unfortunately, these traits are even more present in today's defeated world.

Take a look at the year 2020 when the pandemic became a major part of our lives. In 2020, there were 538,203 violent-crime incidents, and 640,836 offenses reported in the United States.[4] Domestic violence cases increased by 25-33% globally,[5] and anxiety and depression increased by a massive 25% worldwide.[6]

That's only recently.

A Change of Mind and Status

Some might ask if Adam and Eve truly had control over the situation. After all, they were a target. Satan was going to continue pursuing them until he succeeded. This question could be applied to any of us facing a decision to choose one path or the other. The truth is you will always be tempted or pursued when you are following a purposed path; there will always be distractions placed at your feet. You may lose your way and feel as though you are defeated, but remember deceit is the goal of the enemy.

Regroup; gather your strength; know that God loves you and move on. Say this to yourself: *"For I am persuaded, that neither death, nor life, nor angels, nor principalities, nor powers, nor things present, nor things to come, nor height, nor depth, nor any other creature, shall be able to separate [me] from the love of God, which is in Christ Jesus our Lord"* (Romans 8:38-39 KJV).

In addition to speaking biblical affirmations, you should ask yourself, when did you go left when you should have gone right in life? Most likely it was because of deceit. Either you didn't get the whole story or insist on knowing the whole story because the situation might not have ended the way you wanted it to.

There's nothing more powerful than the lies we tell ourselves. If somebody lies to you, you have a choice to believe it or not. But when you lie to yourself, it's harder to combat that kind of untruth because you are personally involved. Remember, lies or deceit were never God's intent for you or Adam.

---

[4] Federal Bureau of Investigation: Crime Data Explorer. (n.d.). Retrieved September 5, 2022, from https://crime-data-explorer.fr.cloud.gov.

[5] Mineo, L. (2022, June 29). Shadow pandemic of domestic violence. *Harvard Gazette.* Retrieved August 17, 2022, from https://news.harvard.edu.

[6] World Health Organization. (n.d.). Covid-19 pandemic triggers 25% increase in prevalence of anxiety and depression worldwide. *World Health Organization.* Retrieved August 17, 2022, from https://www.who.int.

My Own Undefeated Life

My parents cultivated my appetite for the things of God at an early age in my life. So, my belief system was reinforced by what I saw in the lives of my parents and what I experienced in my personal relationship with God. When you are raised knowing the God of love, you get to know Him and appreciate Him for who He is and whom He made you to be. Even with such a strong foundation, I was unable to turn the word defeated into undefeated for my life until I came to an understanding of whom God intended me to be. But that didn't mean I was perfect in any way. I experienced my challenges, but I always had a reason to get back up when I fell, and I could always count on God to return me to a place of purpose. He is a very powerful God!

God's name, Elohim, reflects His sovereignty and absolute power. We are made in His image. This creative concept is also mirrored in familial relationships. Children often look exactly like their parents or grandparents. Not only does God want us to look like Him, but He also freely gives us His power. Earlier we mentioned David's standoff with Goliath. The scrawny guy didn't have the power to defeat a giant the size of Goliath, but with God's help, he did. When you walk confidently in God's power, you have the ability to use so many things to your advantage – even things that might have destroyed others. You decide if you want to choose God and activate that supernatural power in your life. How do I know that? Jesus said so.

There was a video on Instagram about a young lady who was running a race, and she lost her shoe as she came around the track. She lost her position in the race because she went back to retrieve her shoe. Once she put her shoe back on, she returned to the race and started running as if her very life depended on it. At some point, her expertise, training, and skill connected with her desire to win, and she went from last place to first place in a flash. I share this story because when you are a true champion, circumstances can't change your ultimate goal, especially when you are operating in the supernatural power of God. But it's a choice you must make.

You Got the Power

Your decisions are important. Not only do they strike a chord in eternity, but they directly impact what you set out to do in this life. You can accomplish whatever you decide in life if you are aligned with the right power source.

God hardwired you with everything that you need in order to be undefeated. You have been hardwired to pursue God's purpose for your life. You were born into this world with a specific purpose tattooed in your DNA. This purpose fuels your reason for living. To live an undefeated lifestyle, you have to know why you exist. You must have a very important discussion with God and go on an internal treasure hunt to discover your purpose. Once it's identified, you must develop an action plan to pursue it. This is what gives you the fighting power to get back in the race even when you fall into last place because you lost a shoe. Your "Pursuit of Purpose" is critical to establishing a meaningful lifestyle while you are here on earth.

We all have a birth date. A day for each of us will also come when the doctor looks at his watch and says, "Time of death is..." Life and death are some of the only things that we are guaranteed to experience as human beings. Two hundred fifty babies are born every minute in the world.[7] One hundred twenty people die per minute.[8] This may be interesting information, but what's more important is how many of those individuals really live their lives in between those major life occurrences.

---

[7] Guardian News and Media. (2018, April 23). With 250 babies born each minute, how many people can the Earth sustain? *The Guardian*. Retrieved September 5, 2022, from https://www.theguardian.com.
[8] Death rate is 120 per minute. *Bioethics Research Library*. (n.d.). Retrieved September 5, 2022, from https://bioethics.georgetown.edu.

What will those who knew you say about the kind of life you lived when your life here is over? What will God say about the life that you've lived on earth? What would you say if you were required to do your own tribute at your homegoing service? As Dr. Myles Monroe said, " Don't die old; die empty. That's the goal of life." Discover your purpose and live it to the fullest, until there is nothing left to give.

You might say, "Well, I wasn't born with the same opportunities that you had," or "I have this disability that limits my ability to live a normal life," or "I sometimes suffer from bi-polar episodes, so I can't really commit to anything other than survival." Numerous people have the same challenges, but they still managed to live purpose-filled lives. Why? Because they recognized that God had given them the power to live an undefeated life, and they pushed beyond those limitations.

Take Marcus Bowers for an example. He grew up in South Park, Houston. When he was a teenager, he had to prove himself as the new kid when he arrived at Attucks Middle School. Bowers states, "You had to have a certain mindset to survive in that kind of neighborhood. When people know that you will bulldoze through any obstacle that may get in your way, they tend to leave you alone." Living tough was a raw reality for him.

Bowers learned how to reinforce his undefeated status, by following his mother's advice. "If someone hits you, hit them back. And if they are bigger than you, take something and knock the _____ out of them." He took it a step further. If you were aggressive towards him in any way, and you got within arm's reach, he's going to knock you out. He never let anyone hit him first. At that time, he was the personified example of undefeated in the flesh. He never joined a gang or group that made him an adversary to anyone because he was confident in his ability to hold his own in the face of any challenge. He literally fought his way through life, and nobody physically or mentally beat him. At that time, that was how he knew to survive undefeated – until he was introduced to a new way.

Just two weeks after graduating high school, Bowers enlisted in the United States Navy. He learned strategies, techniques, and tactics that enhanced his abilities to the point that he successfully served four years in Naval Special Forces as a Special Warfare Combatant Crewmen (SWCC). The military fine-tuned his method of communication. In the streets, he had to use his fists, but the Navy taught him how to use his words to remain undefeated. This elevated his standard of thinking and living.

Today, Marcus Bowers is an author, comedian entrepreneur, and one of the co-founders of She's Happy Hair, a hair and hair-products business with multiple locations all over the U.S. His undefeated mindset enabled him to start the company with an initial $900 investment and grow it into a multi-million-dollar business without ever taking out a business loan.

Bowers is very dedicated to his work. He combines running a successful business, traveling to different countries and continents in search of products and imports while meeting face to face with overseas factory owners and decision-makers, and performing comedy routines, with serving his community through his non-profit, The She's Happy Foundation. He makes time to help troubled teens realize their potential and build brighter futures. He has been recognized for his accomplishments with various awards and even appearances on ABC and Fox News. However, his primary goal is to give other kids like him a fighting chance to be undefeated, regardless of the obstacles they may face.

How does an individual go from one of the toughest parts of Houston to attain various levels of success? According to Marcus Bowers, "It's a mindset. You are only defeated when you stop," Bowers advises. "No one can defeat you but you!" Marcus Bowers refuses to let any part of his childhood or life hinder him. He is a reminder that you have the power to write your story in any way that you want. When you write it with your purpose in mind, you not only benefit, but the world around you benefits as well.

You might know people who are living for God, but they live in poverty. And when you try to encourage them, they tell you that they have never had anything and won't ever have anything. My response would be, "Yes, they are right." If that is their reality, and they aren't willing to pursue their God-given purpose, that's where they will stay stuck.

Change whatever you need to pursue your God-given purpose. You have the power to do so. The benefit of serving a loving God is that He loves to give us gifts and fulfill His promises in our lives. We simply must choose to live an undefeated life and activate the power He so freely gives to us.

CHAPTER THREE
A Defeatist Mindset

Every new day presents us with an opportunity to win. We wake up with a blank slate to create the kind of day that we desire. But there may be one problem. If our mindset is in failure mode, we are already defeated before our feet hit the floor.

The Battlefield of the Mind

In order to conquer our day, we must first fight and win the battle within. That's impossible when you possess a defeatist attitude. What is a defeatist mindset? It is a negative mindset in which you believe you're going to fail before you even start. You talk yourself out of achieving things by telling yourself you're incapable of success, even if you don't have any evidence to support that. It has a demoralizing, crippling, and immobilizing effect. If left unchecked, it can block you from achieving your most important goals.

Earlier, I talked about my Spring Training experience. My coach's derogatory comments and negative reinforcement weighed on my thinking. He had done it that way for years with remarkable success with other players, but they didn't show up with an undefeated mindset. Remember, my parents had done a tremendous job cultivating a "win no matter what" attitude within me when I was younger. The issue I now faced was hearing the negative reinforcement about me and my performance when I was so used to receiving positive.

In a way, the coach held a position of authority. I looked up to him. I respected his role in my life as a mentor and trainer. I relied on him to be supportive and even motivational. When it didn't happen initially, I began looking for a way out of a game I loved. Why? Because I began to believe the negativity that was thrown my way every day during practice. As a young man, it began to reshape my trajectory. I was headed for the pros, but this man was telling me that I wasn't good enough.

I never fully accepted what the coach said about my performance on the field, but I began to take on a different attitude. The interesting thing about Spring Training was we never played against opposing teams, but I begin to feel like I had lost in a real game. Despite deeply knowing my true skillset and abilities, I slowly began taking on the belief that I wasn't going to win – not with the coach anyway. I gave up and walked away from the game I loved. If we hadn't later talked about the "why" for his training methods, I would never have returned to the team because it would have killed the hope I had inside of me to play football.

The battle in my mind was real.

A Self-Defeating Attack

How many times have you adopted the negativity others said about you before you even got a chance to form your own opinion or get to know what you are destined to be? How often has the negativity played over and over again in your mind, stealing away your destiny?

The Word of God says, "As a man thinketh in his heart, so is he…" Who are you? Do you suffer from low self-esteem? Merriam-Webster defines self-esteem as, "a confidence and satisfaction in oneself." So, if you're not confident or satisfied with yourself you've already lost a battle. This affects the way you view life and everything in it. You may have limited hope as a result, and when setbacks come your way, they can cause devastating chaos in your life. This is a self-defeated mindset, an attack of sorts, and something many people face.

I can't imagine anybody intentionally imposing a defeated mindset on himself or herself. But it is a reality for a lot of people. Several things contribute to it, including the following:

Experiences of failure. Nobody likes to fail, but it is a part of life. How we handle it is key. Research suggests that people with low self-esteem are more negatively affected by failure experiences than those with high self-esteem.[9] After experiencing failure, participants with high self-esteem focus on their strengths and suppress their weaknesses, apparently as a way to maintain their positive self-view by staving off threats to it. On the other hand, those with low self-esteem accessed their weaknesses more after failure. Given how adversely affected they are by setbacks, it's easy to see why people with low self-esteem might develop a defeatist attitude.

Although I was not a part of this research, I can confirm its accuracy through personal experience. I was taught to esteem myself in the Lord. Since He is the King of kings and the Lord of lords, that automatically places me in higher esteem than those who are not. That said, I often resort to exactly what the research states to combat any negative or discouraging encounters I have. Rather than accepting what I feel might distort how God sees me or the positive aspects I know about myself, I cling to my Heavenly Father's loving perspective of me. I am "[God's] workmanship created for good works,"[10] so I am built to withstand hardships and even faced failures. Indeed, I am esteemed in the Lord.

I cannot account for how a person with low self-esteem would respond to failure. However, I can sympathize and offer encouragement. I can say with confidence that your failure does not define you. You are a child of the Most High. God sees you as worthy of His grace and love despite your failure.

Negative past experiences. Another thing that may cultivate a defeatist attitude are negative past experiences. Scripture tells us that anyone born of a woman has few days to live, and those days are full of trouble (Job 14:1). Unfortunately, there is no way around hurtful experiences; they come with the task of living. Being children of God does not protect us from experiencing hurt and pain.

---

[9] Dodgson, P. G., & Wood, J. V. (1998). Self-esteem and the cognitive accessibility of strengths and weaknesses after failure. *Journal of Personality and Social Psychology*, 75(1), 178–197. https://doi.org/10.1037/0022-3514.75.1.178.
[10] Ephesians 2:10 ESV

Painful events can make you avoid future situations where you might fail again. This was true for me. I did not want to face another football practice only to receive more badgering. I dreaded watching films of the practice where my faults were constantly on replay. It was like pouring salt in a fresh wound the coach had created. If I am honest, I still hesitate at times when I know I am about to face a painful experience. Think about it. Who wants to continue experiencing hurt?

Negative past experiences coupled with low self-esteem can breed a paralyzing fear of failure that stops you from achieving your goals. This is something we definitely do not want. That's why it is important to reflect on past experiences, learn from them, and grow as a result of them.

Peer pressure. The wrong peer influence can also negatively affect your attitude about yourself. In a consumer study, participants were given a product and were allowed to form their own opinions of it. But when they were later told what their peers thought of the same product, negative external opinions exerted a much stronger influence over their attitudes than positive ones. While you're certainly not a consumer product, other people's opinions of you can be a product of your negative self-view.

One of the most powerful tools in our arsenal to defeat negativity is to be selective about who you are around. You must be around what you want! It doesn't matter where you originated, what matters is where you end up. To develop an undefeated mindset, you must align your thinking, reading, speaking, and friendships with where you want to be. The moral of this story is, "Your friends determine your future." Choose them wisely.

Core beliefs. You may even have negative core beliefs about yourself and life. Core beliefs are what we believe about ourselves, others, and the world around us, such as "people are generally kind" or

"I'm not good enough." Whether we're conscious of them or not, core beliefs affect our behavior and explain why we do what we do. For example, if one of your core beliefs is "I ruin everything..." You'll fall prey to what psychologists call "confirmation bias" – you'll start looking for evidence that supports your negative core belief. This can perpetuate a defeatist attitude that may be holding you back from living life to the fullest.

Because this self-defeating attack is internal, you would think that others would not notice it, but most of the time they do. Here are a few visible effects of a defeatist attitude:

Unpleasant appearance and presence. Have you ever seen the comic strip *Peanuts* by the late Charles M. Schulz? There is a fictional character named Pig-Pen, a little boy who is extremely dirty and followed by a permanent cloud of dust. When the others see him arrive on the scene, they ultimately have to pull out a tissue or handkerchief to cover their noses. Nobody said it to him on the show, but Pig-Pen was filthy, smelly, and quite uncomfortable to be around. A defeatist attitude can make others view you like they did Pig-Pen because of the negativity that you carry around.

Fail-prone positioning. A defeatist attitude puts you in a position to fail more than the average person. In an ironic twist, a defeatist attitude – so often used as a shield against failure – can actually make you more prone to failure. When your self-talk consists of statements like, "I can't do this" or "I'm going to fail," you can become a self-fulfilling prophecy. That negativity can cause you to lose your competitive edge and positioning.[11]

It also prevents you from trying new things by practicing self-efficacy. Psychologist Albert Bandura defined self-efficacy as "an individual's belief in his or her capacity to execute behaviors necessary to produce specific performance attainments."[12] In his research, he found that people with low self-efficacy were more likely to avoid challenging situations and were more likely to give up.

As if things couldn't get any worse on the inside, negative opinions from the outside compound the problem Not only do they shift opinions from good to bad, but they also make bad ones even worse.[13]

When you come out of the womb, you are innocent and clean. That's why people love to smell babies because they smell like clean clothes after a spin in the dryer, but better. But as you grow up, you have negative thoughts, form negative opinions, adopt the negative opinions of others, and are negatively spoken of. Imagine yourself walking around with negative signs all over your body that are telling people who you are and what you are about. This is how a defeated person looks. You may think that sharing your stuff with others helps you to play it safe, but it could set you up for someone to hurt and manipulate you.

Combatting Self-Defeat
A defeatist mindset might not be something any of us aim for or desires, but it sometimes finds its way into our thoughts, minds, and hearts. If left unchecked, it could adversely affect several areas of our lives. What's important is how to ward it off and keep it at bay. We can do this by resetting our thinking. God tells us to "transform our minds." That's exactly what it takes to combat a mindset of defeat.

For example, my daughter failed a spelling test. She began to speak negatively about herself. She said she wasn't smart, that she was nothing. Good for nothing. Stupid. So, she told my wife the story. Then her mother realized she had written down all of the stuff I

[11] Van Raalte, J. L., Cornelius, A. E., Brewer, B. W., & Hatten, S. J. (2000). The antecedents and consequences of self-talk in competitive tennis. *Journal of Sport and Exercise Psychology*, 22(4), 345–356. https://doi.org/10.1123/jsep.22.4.345.
[12] Bandura, A. (1977). Self-efficacy: Toward a unifying theory of behavioral change. *Psychological Review*, 84(2), 191–215. https://doi.org/10.1037/0033-295x.84.2.191.
[13] Sen, S., & Lerman, D. (2007). Why are you telling me this? an examination into negative consumer reviews on the web. *Journal of Interactive Marketing*, 21(4), 76–94. https://doi.org/10.1002/dir.20090.

typed above on the back of her test. When my wife gave me the paper, God told me I had to intervene. When I got home, I took her by the fireplace and turned it on. I told her that these were lies the Devil told her. I told her we never speak evil about ourselves. I reinforced what I said by telling her, "You are a Child of God, fearfully and wonderfully made!" Then we took the words and wrote them on a new piece of paper and burned the paper that was full of negativity. We sent those words back to hell where they originated. Later, we studied the words and she passed. The purpose of the fireplace experience was to etch that moment in her head and confirm the fact that she was everything good. I convinced her that we should never call ourselves *nothing*. We hugged and got back to living an undefeated life. She had a complete mind reset and was reacquainted with her undefeated heritage.

The same way I rerouted my daughter's thinking is the same way God encourages us to transform our minds so that our thoughts and actions will move from a level of sabotage to ones that rise and soar. I call it cultivating a culture of undefeated inclusiveness. This means surrounding yourself with the spirit of success and the type of people who promote a relentless standard way of living. In other words, become what you want to be and attract more of it to your immediate space. This must be intentional through calculated moves. In order to cultivate a culture of undefeated inclusiveness, you often have to create one.

I try to help with this by modeling the role of an entrepreneur and building communities of individuals with the purpose to improve their current circumstances. I created quarterly meetings on GroupMe to help people get free of financial bondage. I started helping them with taxes and mortgages, arming them with the knowledge to make room for an undefeated mentality.

As a pastor, I felt that the church must take some responsibility for helping its community of believers to prosper. I took the necessary action to help people by not only modeling an undefeated attitude as an entrepreneur but also sharing the principles necessary to break that cycle of poverty in their lives. Here are five of the strategies that I used to help them overcome a defeatist attitude:

1. Remember that you're doing something hard. Entrepreneurs are the people who create new things, take risks, and imagine new worlds. That's hard, and mistakes and stumbling blocks will happen. If it weren't hard, everyone would be an entrepreneur. The key is to stop beating yourself up about it when a failure occurs. Try practicing a bit of compassion with yourself Dr. Kristin Neff says, "Instead of mercilessly judging and criticizing yourself for various inadequacies or shortcomings, self-compassion means you are kind and understanding when confronted with personal failings."[14] Learning self-compassion is the first step to helping you move on from failure effectively.

2. Re-route your self-talk. Negative self-talk as a response to failure can be a major roadblock in overcoming setbacks – things like: "I'm a failure." "I'm such an idiot." "This will never work." "This is too hard." This kind of talk spells bad news for people trying to achieve their goals. According to Dr. Jennice Vilhauer, "... we all have an automatic selective filtering system that will look for evidence in our environment that matches up with whatever we believe to be true about ourselves. We will then disregard other evidence to the contrary."[15] Your expectations create your circumstances,[16] which means we tend to zero in on small mistakes and errors as proof that we're stupid or that our dreams will never become reality. In other words, you will rise no higher than you believe you will.

3. Embrace failure by identifying which emotions are holding you back. People are encouraged to "learn from failure" so much that the phrase "embrace failure" is a cliché, but it's a cliché for a reason. Learning to embrace failure and taking an analytical rather than an emotional approach is a huge step in overcoming a defeatist mindset. Dr. Melinda Fouts identifies the fact that:

- "The emotions that arise during a failure and can hold you captive to defeat embarrassment, frustration, anger, regret, nausea, fear of failure and judgment or feeling like you are inadequate."
- Negative emotions that come from a feeling of failure or defeat can magnify or create other problems, making it difficult not to take failure personally.
- Here are her tips for overcoming negative emotions:
    - Adopt a positive, flexible, and curious mindset rather than a fixed one by thinking "this attempt didn't work, so I'll try another approach that does."
    - Recognize the negative emotions that arise from failure, so they don't have such a powerful hold over you
    - Deal with past failures to improve self-esteem and confidence
    - Disassociate the idea of "failure" from the idea of "defeat." You haven't failed, but rather, as the famous quote attributed to Thomas Edison goes, "You've found 10,000 ways that don't work."[17]

To overcome a defeatist mindset, take a magnifying glass to what's holding you back as well as what motivates you. Work on your grit and tenacity (it can be learned!) to focus on your long-term goals and remember that entrepreneurs survive and thrive by being self-aware about what motivates them and by cultivating an agile mindset. Agility is key when battling

---

[14] Neff, K. (2022, January 21). Self-Compassion. Retrieved September 3, 2022, from https://self-compassion.org/
[15] Vilhauer, J. (2016, March 18). 4 ways to stop beating yourself up, Once and for all. Psychology Today. Retrieved September 3, 2022, from https://www.psychologytoday.com.
[16] TEDxTalks. (2015). Why you don't get what you want; It's not what you expect." YouTube. Retrieved July 20, 2022, from https://www.youtube.com/watch?v=FwLeiY5f7sI.
[17] Is your defeatist attitude keeping you down? Here's how to stop self-defeating thoughts. (n.d.). Retrieved July 23, 2022, from https://www.fingerprintforsuccess.com.

4. Consider the consequences of worst-case scenarios. People with a defeatist attitude tend to catastrophize, meaning they imagine the worst possible outcome. If that's you, flip this bad habit on its head and use it to your advantage. To begin, ask yourself, "What's the worst that could happen?" and allow yourself to run through worst-case scenarios. So, for example, let's say you're catastrophizing about giving a presentation at an important work conference. You might think: "What if I forget what I should say next?" What if there's a technical difficulty?" "What if everyone hates my presentation?"

But don't stop there! Now that you've got your list of worst-case scenarios. Ask yourself another question, "What's most likely to happen, though?" This will help balance your negative thinking with more realistic thoughts and even a plan of action. You might counter your previous "what if" statements with: "I'll bring note cards, so even if I forget what to say next, I can find it in my notes." "I've been to this conference several times before, and no one's ever had a technical difficulty, so it's unlikely to happen." "My colleagues have shown a lot of interest in the topic of my presentation, so they probably wouldn't hate it."

And lastly, ask yourself, "If the worst-case scenario were to happen, how would I cope with it?" This allows you to see that the worst-case scenario you fear would likely not be as life-altering as you initially assumed. "Well, even if I forget what I was going to say next, I can just move on to the next slide." "Even if my mic cuts out or something, they've got technicians who could get me another mic, or I could just project my voice more." "Even if my colleagues hate the presentation, I doubt they'd tell me. And if someone says something mean, it would hurt, but it wouldn't matter to me a year from now. I'd move on." And if your worst-case scenario comes true – take heart. Try not to dwell on momentary setbacks. Remember, they are short-lived and mostly designed as learning experiences that eventually fade, not fixtures of defeat.

5. Celebrate the small wins. Expecting outstanding results the first time you attempt something new is unrealistic and sets you up for failure. To overcome your defeatist attitude, you want to gather more evidence that you can succeed. To do that, start with small, manageable goals. For example, maybe you want to launch a six-figure consulting business. If you expect you're going to be on track for your revenue goal within a month of getting started, you're bound to be disappointed. Instead, break that goal up into smaller milestones. Focus first on winning your first client. And when that happens, treat yourself! Little by little, as you accumulate more small successes, your self-confidence should grow, and your defeatist attitude should diminish. In fact, researchers, Teresa Amabile and Steven Kramer, coined the term "progress principle" to describe the fact that making progress tends to boost emotions and motivation.[18]

A Champion's Prerogative

You may not be one hundred percent certain that your goals will be accomplished, but that shouldn't hinder your optimism or pursuit of them. When putting forth efforts to reach those goals, take that as an opportune time to develop an unrelenting drive to move forward. What I am trying to say is the will to be undefeated becomes the champion's prerogative no matter what.

Sometimes combatting a mindset of defeat begins with the simple act of affirming who you are and what you are trying to accomplish, especially if your goal is something that nobody else in your immediate family or circle has achieved or one that others doubt you can attain. This is necessary when you aspire to rise above previous experiences that could adversely affect your future. This was the case for Isaac Moore.

---

[18] Amabile, T. and S. Kramer. *The Progress Principle Using Small Wins to Ignite Joy, Engagement, and Creativity at Work*. Brilliance Audio, 2012.

Moore was raised by a mother who was a drug addict. He and his sister lived that life until he was forced to leave it behind. He became homeless and started living on the streets during his high school years. He will unashamedly take you to the shotgun house he used to live in as a boy in 3rd Ward, Houston, and point out his favorite park bench where he spent many nights staring up at the stars. Not wondering where his next meal would come from but imagining his designs on a runway during Paris Fashion Week. See, he knew at an early age he was called to be a designer, and every penny he got went to forward his career, even as a homeless teen. When his pockets were empty, he would share his vision with anyone who would listen.

In his short 37 years, Moore has overcome great adversity to rack up several accomplishments as a fashion designer, entrepreneur, and student of life. The son of a drug-dealing father and a drug-addicted mother, Isaac Moore recognized very early that if he and his younger sister chose to make anything of their lives, it would have to be independent of their parents. Largely raising himself, Isaac Moore vehemently avoided the culture of illicit drug and alcohol abuse as well as the criminal activity it spawns. He graduated from Jack Yates High School and went on to seek a degree in Marketing at Texas Southern University. The road from orphaned ghetto kid to accomplished fashion designer has been painstakingly hard. From homelessness, burglary, unscrupulous business associates, and just rotten luck, Isaac has endured much in his pursuit of success. For many people, losing everything, and having to sleep in vacant cars and park benches drives them to further despair. For Isaac Moore, it's only inspired him to keep a consistent fire burning under his desired goals.

With the "gift of gab," undying determination, and his noticeable sense of fashion, Isaac Moore decided to stop the generational downfall of his ancestors by becoming and mastering the role of an undefeated champion in his industry. Moore's greatest achievement thus far has been to recognize that his mission in life is not to accept the circumstances into which he was born, but to visualize, understand, and strive to become more, leaving an indelible imprint on the world.

There's power in prayer," Moore states. "I've been out here on my own for a long time, and God has always sustained me." He continues, "I'm so blessed to have even made it this far, especially when others expected me to fail or to follow in my parents' footsteps."

Realizing that dreams do come true with hard work and dedication, Moore continues and encourages others to do the same. His motto in life is, "If you want to make a difference, you have to do things differently." Moore approaches life every day with this in mind, "I am the man I was born to be," and the fashion world is better because of his resilience and undefeated mindset. It's not unusual to see him on Instagram delivering a "big, gift-wrapped box" to celebrities with a tailormade design specialized to complement their brand. It's an experience that often leaves its recipients in tears. Isaac Moore, the designer, is changing lives and making the world a better place, one big box at a time.

Isaac Moore had a strategy for winning regardless of his misfortune and that led to his success. He was careful about what he told himself about his future and quick to eliminate anything that pulled his attention in a different direction. He closed all doors that took him away from his dream and refused to use his words to tear down the delicate staircase that led him to his imminent success. This is what contributes to him being an undefeated champion.

Like Moore, we will have to strategize for our unique situations if we are going to live an undefeated life. I even had to develop a strategy to become the best athlete possible, when winning wasn't enough. This taught me that success starts with the right mindset. As you move through the pages of this book, it is my goal to get you fired up to take action. When you've got the power, potential, and positive attitude necessary to live a life of abundance, the sky's the limit.

Are you ready to defeat your defeatist attitude? Hopefully, by now you realize that you are not doomed to a life of defeatism – your attitude is changeable! Like most things worthwhile, though, it'll take some work. The first step is to become more self-aware, which, congrats, you're already doing!

Repeat after me, I will succeed!

CHAPTER FOUR
A Defeatist Mindset –
Where It All Started

Growing up I was taught to consider how my actions might affect others. Children naturally don't consider the long-term impact or consequences of their actions. Now looking back at that time in my life, I thought and spoke as a child. Many times, I was ignorant and unable to consider the possible impact of my words or actions on the feelings of others.

Even as adults it is easy to underestimate our influence on others and our environment. This also applies to our creations.

Ideas, dreams, and goals are first created in our minds. We envision a thing, come up with a plan, get the resources to do it, and then create it. We then sit back and admire what we created with a sense of satisfaction. Just like a mind can be used for creating good things, it can also be used to create bad things.

The First Curse of Humanity
Remember our earlier discussion of the Garden of Eden? One bad thought took down all of humanity. That one thought has negatively influenced generations from the beginning of time. Comedian, Flip Wilson's quote, "The devil made me do it!" relates to Eve. I could imagine her saying this as an excuse for eating the forbidden fruit in the garden, and it has been the patented excuse for having a defeatist mindset ever since.

Think about the effect this attitude has on creation. We see evidence of its ruin all over the world. There's a worldwide pandemic, wars, poverty, racism, corruption, food and housing insecurity, and systematic abuse to name a few outcomes. These outcomes are a result of generations of curses. You see, Satan's intent in the Garden of Eden was not to just derail God's plan for all of humanity, but to make us pay for being God's favorite children. He wanted us to feel the same pain he has because he lost his crown as one of the major angels in Heaven. So, he traps us into a defeatist mindset and adds pressure to keep us there as a result of that attitude.

What is a curse? A curse is the opposite of a blessing; whereas a blessing is a pronouncement of good fortune because one is initiated into God's plans, a curse is a pronouncement of ill fortune because one opposes God's plans. God may curse a person or a whole nation because of their opposition to his will.[19]

The first curse of humanity started in the Garden of Eden. God said to Adam, *"Because you listened to your wife and ate from the tree about which I commanded you, `You must not eat of it,' Cursed is the ground because of you; through painful toil, you will eat of it all the days of your life. It will produce thorns and thistles for you, and you will eat the plants of the field"* (Genesis 3:17 NIV).

Generational Curses of a Family

Generational curses are the result of the unrepentant sins of our forefathers and mothers. According to Dr. Wave Nunnally, "Satan has the right to continue to hold a legal claim against Christians who have not effectively dealt with their generational curses, resulting in failure, violence, impotence, profanity, obesity, poverty, shame, sickness, grief, fear, and even physical death."[20] As I contemplated generational curses and their cause, I asked myself why do physicians ask about family history when accessing a diagnosis for medical treatment. A person's ancestry can tell a lot about their predisposition for certain kinds of health challenges. There are generational habits, patterns, and belief systems that transfer from one generation to the next.

Family-level influences on health derive from three main sources: genetics, a shared physical environment, and a shared social environment. Think of it this way. Whatever flows in the bloodline naturally shows up in subsequent generations. Parents pass on

---

[19] Cline, A. (2019, June 25). Curses and cursing: What is a curse? Learn Religions. Retrieved August 4, 2022, from https://www.learnreligions.com.
[20] Nunnally, W. (2007). Generational curses: The sins of generational curses. Bible Unplugged. Retrieved September 4, 2022, from https://wavenunnally.com.

traits or characteristics to their children, such as eye color and blood type. Some health conditions and diseases can be passed on genetically too. Sometimes, one characteristic has many different forms. For example, blood type can be A, B, AB, or O. That's why one of your relatives might say you have a certain physical feature like your mother, father, or one of your grandparents.

Likewise, a family that lives under the same roof typically eats the same thing, communicates in a specific way, and socializes with a connected community. These things directly impact an individual's way of thinking and living.

Generational Curses and My Family
Generational cohorts pass on inheritable patterns and habits that can also produce mindsets of defeat. This is also personal for me because I wasn't automatically exempt. It took the efforts of my father and grandfather to protect me from experiencing the worst of what my predecessors passed down. Allow me to explain.

My father is a native Louisianan. He grew up in the 1960s in Deridder around the time when racial tensions were high. As a young boy, he experienced a neutrally divided perspective on racial tensions in his household. On one hand, he observed his father who was accepted among whites due to his popularity in sports, baseball in particular. On the other hand, his mother was a devoted Christian and churchgoer, who was deeply fearful of the racial tensions which existed around them.

While both his parents provided a safe and sufficient lifestyle for him and his siblings, his father's physical abuse, alcoholism, and absence in the home weighed heavy on his desire to be different, and better when he grew up. My father didn't allow the negative impact of what he observed in his family to dictate the constructs of his dreams for success and family. As a young child, he clearly remembers a promise he made to himself – to never be like his father. He kept that promise. He is still the backbone of a God-fearing family that thrives because of faith and love.

Growing up in the 60s was very much different from the life that my father was able to provide for me. He did what he said, despite the circumstances he grew up in. He changed the generational construct. In fact, he and all of his siblings escaped the construct of the generational curse of abuse, alcoholism, and a father's absence.

He also grappled with the reality and terror of racism. The era in which my father was born was very different from my era. Although my father's generation was different from his father's, one commonality existed. They lived a constant life of fear and fighting for rights to what should have been available to them as natural-born citizens. It was a time when injustice was on everyone's mind. The struggles against racism and segregation entered the mainstream of life. My grandparents lived out of the hand dealt to them. Their freedoms were limited and fair conditions were few.

The family experience during this time hinged on faith in God on both sides of the racial barriers. Civil rights looked very different on both sides. Some Whites prayed to God for separation; most Blacks prayed to God for inclusion. At the end of the battle, separation was defeated, and inclusion won. God's will for humanity shall forever remain undefeated.

Generations of Change (A Historical Narrative)
A growing group of Americans spoke out against inequality and injustice during the 1950s. Injustice was deliberately rooted in laws; several fell under the guise of Jim Crow. Jim Crow was a series of laws that relegated Blacks to a substandard way of living – one that society approved and expected Blacks to also accept. How many of you know that just because something is written as the law doesn't make it right with God?

African Americans had been fighting against racial discrimination for centuries. During the 1950s, however, the struggle against racism and segregation entered the mainstream of American life. For example, in 1954, in the landmark Brown v. Board of Education case, the Supreme Court declared that "separate educational facilities" for black children were "inherently unequal." This ruling was the first nail in Jim Crow's coffin.

Who in their scripturally sound mind would think that God approves of one superior race? If you think about the fact that Jesus went out of his way and traveled to Samaria (where a "stigmatized" race of people lived) to personally meet and minister to the woman at the well, you know His position on the issue of racial discrimination or injustice, Moreover, Jesus chose to die so that salvation is free for people of every race, creed, and color. How could anyone ever conclude that He respects one race over another?

Some people did though. In fact, Many Southern whites resisted the Brown ruling. They adamantly defended their children's privileged school careers. They withdrew their children from public schools and enrolled them in all-white "segregation academies," and they used violence and intimidation to prevent blacks from asserting their rights. In 1956, more than 100 Southern congressmen even signed a "Southern Manifesto" declaring that they would do all they could to defend segregation.

Despite these efforts, a new movement was born. In December 1955, a Montgomery activist named Rosa Parks was arrested for refusing to give her seat on a city bus to a white person. Her arrest sparked a thirteen-month boycott of the city's buses by its black citizens, which only ended when the bus companies stopped discriminating against African American passengers. Acts of "nonviolent resistance" like the boycott helped shape the civil rights movement of the next decade.

Many generations fought for everyone's rights so that younger generations would have a better quality of life. Some people actively fought, while others stood peacefully and faithfully waited for God to show up. You and I currently reap those benefits of the battle that God won. We live in a time when black children sit in an integrated classroom. That privilege came about because many people sacrificed.

The Young Challenger for Change

Among the people I just mentioned and many others who made the conscious decision to endure hardships for the benefit of others were Ruby Bridges and her family. Her parents agreed to take the risk, and Ruby Bridges made small steps in a huge journey each day. Those small steps amounted to a life-changing event during my father's upbringing that changed the American educational system.

Ruby Bridges is proof that nobody is too young to challenge the status quo and radically shift an existing societal standard. At the tender age of six, Ruby Bridges advanced the cause of civil rights in November 1960 when she became the first African American student to integrate an elementary school in the South.

Bridges proved her intelligence by passing an entrance exam for African American students to see whether they could compete academically at the all-white school. She qualified to attend. There were advantages to attending this school. For one, it would be convenient. With the school only a few blocks from her home, the ride would be shorter. Plus, she could learn with her white peers despite previous segregation laws.

However, her parents were torn about whether to let her attend the all-white William Frantz Elementary School. Her father resisted, fearing for his daughter's safety, but her mother wanted their daughter to have the educational opportunities that her parents had been denied. Meanwhile, the school district dragged its feet, delaying her admittance. Other Black students, who qualified to attend, decided not to leave their school at all. The other three were sent to the all-white McDonough Elementary School.

Four federal marshals escorted Bridges and her mother to the school every day that year. She walked past crowds screaming vicious slurs at her. Undeterred, she later said she only became frightened when she saw a woman holding a black baby doll in a coffin.[21] Her terrifying journey continued after her mother left her at the school to learn each day. She spent her first day in the principal's office due to the chaos created as angry white parents pulled their children from school. Ardent segregationists withdrew their children permanently. Barbara Henry, a white Boston native, was the only teacher willing to accept her. All year, the young Bridges was a class of one. She ate lunch alone and sometimes played with her teacher at recess. This child risked her mental, emotional, and physical safety. But she never missed a day of school that year.

While some supported her bravery – and some northerners sent money to aid her family – others protested throughout the city. The Bridges family suffered for their courage. Ruby's father lost his job, and grocery stores refused to sell to her mother. Her share-cropping grandparents were evicted from the farm where they had lived for a quarter-century. Ruby Bridges eventually graduated from a desegregated high school and went on to live a very successful life. As you can see it was not without hardships due to racially plagued systems and thinking passed down from previous generations.

Ruby Bridges said the following:
  Each and every one of us is born with a clean heart. Our babies

[21] Michals, D. (2015). Ruby Bridges. *National Women's History Museum*. Retrieved July 27, 2022, from https://www.womenshistory.org.

know nothing about hate or racism. But soon they begin to learn – and only from us. We keep racism alive. We pass it on to our children. We owe it to our children to help them keep their clean slate.[22]

Bridges and her family fought to protect the innocence of children from the brutal bias and hate of racism. They confronted those shared systems, persevered through subsequent hardships, and courageously created opportunities for individuals to travel a path not established by an oppressive origin.

Several generations joined efforts to eliminate racism. We can look down through the years where generations have made valiant attempts, and in a lot of cases succeeded, against the wretched intent of racial injustice. Although there has been progress, and some of its effects have been reduced, the distorted viewpoint still exists on different levels. Thus, the work remains, and we must be vigilant in the peaceful fight against it. We owe it to the betterment of humanity.

---

[22] McCluskey, E. (2002, April 25). Ruby Bridges evokes tears, smiles as she tells her tale." Harvard Gazette. Retrieved July 20, 2022, from https://news.harvard.edu.

Generational curses are anchors that weigh on potential progress and stunt growth. But they are never cemented into any one family's DNA or affixed into an individual's destiny. They should be thought of as fixtures that can be moved aside and even eliminated. We choose. Either we struggle with the weight of anchors or find and utilize tools to break these curses.

The Curse of Poverty

I know this is a lot of information to digest, but the best way to truly understand poverty as a struggle is to educate. Poverty itself is a sensitive subject and should be approached with the utmost care. Personally, my experience with poverty is limited, and I consider myself truly blessed. However, as a Christian leader, I must assist in community outreach, and this is an area that is near and dear to my heart. It has become kind of a crusade of mine.

There are staggering statistics related to poverty. From the 1950s to 2010, married couple families dropped from two-thirds of all households to less than half. Most troubling is the rapid rise in single parenthood, which is associated with higher levels of poverty.[23] Unlike in the past, there is no "typical" US family today.

In the late 1950s, the poverty rate was approximately 22%, with just shy of 40 million Americans living in poverty. However, poverty is now a global problem. According to the World Bank in 2015, over 700 million people were living on less than $1.90 a day.[24] While that represents a milestone (in 1990, it was over one billion), that's still way too many people. That number also includes extreme poverty, which is defined by the United Nations as "a condition characterized by severe deprivation of basic human needs, including food, safe drinking water, sanitation facilities, health, shelter, education, and information. It depends not only on income but also on access to services."[25]

---

[23] Schulte, B. (2021, October 23). Unlike in the 1950s, there is no 'typical' U.S. family today. *The Washington Post.* Retrieved July 28, 2022, from https://www.washingtonpost.com.
[24] World Bank Group. (2018, September 19). Decline of global extreme poverty continues but has slowed. *World Bank.* Retrieved September 5, 2022, from https://www.worldbank.org.
[25] United Nations. (2022, July 20). PAWSSD Chapter 2 | DISD. *United Nations.* Retrieved September 5, 2022, from https://www.un.org.

So, what causes poverty in the first place? Here are ten root causes:[26]

#1. **Lack of good jobs/job growth.** This is the main reason people think of when analyzing poverty, and rightfully so. It remains an issue in several countries, including the United States. In many countries, there are not enough jobs to go around. In the United States, people who work do not receive adequate compensation, so they still live below federal poverty guidelines.

#2: **Lack of good education.** The second root cause of poverty is a lack of education. It contributes to the cycle of poverty because it is passed down from one generation to another. The likelihood of a generation without proper education receiving tools to change their situation for the better is slim.

#3: **Warfare/conflict.** War brings everything to a halt, including productivity that fuels the economy. Revitalizing the economy and getting people back to work takes time. It also takes a toll on working families.

#4: **Weather/climate change.** According to the World Bank, "climate change has the power to impoverish 100 million people in the next decade or so." Extreme conditions such as drought, floods, and severe storms, can adversely affect thriving countries and further damage struggling ones.

#5: **Social injustice.** Gender discrimination, racism, or other forms of social injustice, are often antecedents of poverty. People who are victims of social injustice struggle with gaining access to opportunities and resources that can change their impoverished state.

---

[26] Soken-Huberty, E. (2022, April 24). "10 common root causes of poverty. *Human Rights Careers*. Retrieved July 26, 2022, from https://www.humanrightscareers.com.

#6:   Lack of food and water. These essentials must be met if a person possesses the strength to hold a job and earn money. Lack of these two things will leave a person malnourished and more susceptible to illnesses, which further complicates the situation.

#7:   Lack of infrastructure. Infrastructure such as roads, bridges, the internet, public transport, etc. is important because they make getting to places and information more accessible. Without proper infrastructure, some people miss out on services and resources that would better their situations and life as a whole.

#8:   Lack of government support. The government has the power and resources to resolve many of the described issues. However, many governments neglect to serve the poor. If a government fails to address the needs of the poor, the cycle will continue for certain individuals.

#9:   Lack of good healthcare. Everyone doesn't have access to proper healthcare because of how much it costs. Ironically, people who fall below a certain income bracket cannot afford health and ironically suffer from health issues. Oftentimes, these individuals must choose between paying for medical attention or food.

#10: High costs. Everything is so expensive, even the most basic necessities. Some households spend over sixty percent of their earnings on food. Prices in the housing market continue to rise with inflation. As the cost of these necessities rises, income remains insufficiently low for many.

A poverty mindset is not about how much money a person can make. Nor is it about how much money a person has in the bank. It's about a person's thoughts and perceptions about money which shape their decisions and beliefs. Someone with a poverty mindset sees a surplus in resources as an opportunity for increased consumption, and they often center their efforts on making immediate positive changes. In contrast, a person with a mentality of abundance focuses on using the excess to create momentum that causes future gains.

The Curse of Pride

You know how we sometimes face obstacles that we convince ourselves we can handle? Instead of talking to God and surrendering the situation or problem to Him, we struggle without Him, trying to rely solely on our own feeble strength. Why do we set ourselves up for defeat? Why not run the race with God?

Rejecting strength from the Almighty is negligent and downright foolish. Get rid of your stinking thinking, pride, low self-esteem, fear, generational curses, etc. Join a winning team. It requires your obedience, loyalty, trust, and total submission to His plan for your life.

Pride can also lead to a defeatist attitude. After the great battle of Jericho, God frowned on Israel, His chosen people. They did not follow His instructions because of pride. God told Joshua and his army not to take anything from Jericho that was to be devoted to Him. A man named Achan ignored the Lord's directive. God became enraged at the blatant disrespect of His command and withdrew His protection from them at their next battle. Joshua sent a smaller regiment of soldiers out to fight the smaller city of men, and they lost miserably. Joshua cried out to the Lord. The Lord told Joshua about the devoted and cursed things that were hidden in the camp. He requested that they be found and the guilty party be destroyed. Eventually, Achan admitted his sin and everything that had been stolen, including the gold and silver, and other things

CARLOS JONES II   UNDEFEATED

of value were given to Joshua. Achan and his entire family were stoned to death for their sin and burned as commanded by God.

God is righteous, and when we don't follow His commands, we cut ourselves off from His blessings. Generations before you may have disobeyed God's commandments and positioned your family like Achan positioned his, for utter destruction.

You may see the directives of God as restricting and old-fashioned, but they will literally save your life if you let them. God had a good plan for the children of Israel. They knew that their God always delivered, but the few who did not understand who their God really was, or respected His power, or trusted His word poisoned the entire camp. That's how a defeatist attitude can ruin a people group, country, or nation. When a defeatist mindset is adopted as the norm, utter destruction can have its way.

Breaking Generational Curses
I've shared a lot of information. You might wonder what all of it has to do with you. Basically, I provided a brief history of where generational curses started. You could be the key to where they end. It starts with a simple decision, one that local Houston resident and everyday undefeated champion, Dr. Barbara Walker-Green made.

Hearing or seeing the title "Dr." might make you think this phenomenal woman has always had it together and easily keeps it together. But that is not entirely true. An undeniable shero, Dr. Walker-Green honestly and transparently reveals how a series of intentional decisions make up her path from what could have been undesirable circumstances (imposed on previous generations) to now daily walking an undefeated life and empowering women to do the same.

The realization that "life doesn't have to be like this" and personal choices to do something to change the situation altered the trajectory of self-doubt, and financial instability that her previous generations struggled with. Dr. Walker-Green witnessed her hard-working mother work tirelessly to provide for her children. She remembers:

> My dad died when I was twelve. He left a nice pension that kept the roof over our heads and food, but that was pretty much it. My mom had seven little mouths to feed. She had to do the only work she knew how to do; that was cleaning houses. One day she took me to work with her, as she often did. She was in one room, and I was in another room. She got unusually quiet. When I went to check on her, I found her asleep with her head resting on the table. She was so tired from working all day and then having to go home, feed, and prepare for seven kids. It wasn't easy on her.

Seeing her mother working herself into exhaustion sparked something within the young Dr. Walker-Green. That spark caused her to think about the abilities she had seen within her mother. Even though her mother lived through a time when she was oppressed by society's subpar expectations for African-Americans and women, Dr. Walker-Green knew her mother possessed undefeated capabilities. She reflects on the unrecognized strength of her mother:

At that time some men had the tendency to keep women scared of them just to keep women in line. My mother was one of those women. She jumped at her own shadow most of the time. She didn't really voice her strength and her opinion very much. I knew both were there because, in the conversations that we would have sometimes, I could hear things in her that were very powerful, but she would always back away. She never really reached out and grabbed at a different kind of future. She kind of just went along with the flow of what society expected her to do and be.

Little did her mother know, she had given birth to a rising shero who began a journey of inspiring others with the very woman who had given birth. This preteen motivated her mother to challenge her situation. Dr. Walker-Green remembers the very day she encouraged her mother to strive for more:

> I said, "Mom, you know what, you're not doing this anymore." She just looked at me like, *Girl, what are you talking about?* I said, "You're not doing this anymore; you can do better than this. You don't have to clean people's houses." She asked, "What do you think I should do?" I mean, she literally sat there looking at me – barely a teenager, like we were equal in age wondering what I could do to help. She started crying because she didn't want to do that kind of work. It wore her out. She was tired all the time and I said "We going to go out; we're going to find you a job. I know you can find something where you're not working so hard."

This required courage, something her mother needed to be coached through. And her daughter provided just that. " I know you can do it," the young Dr. Walker-Green said to her mother. "Just believe in yourself." Dr. Walker-Green's positive reinforcements and guidance led her mother in searching for, interviewing for, and getting a different job that utilized her talents and didn't require labor-intensive work. Her mother felt so accomplished because she attained a goal she had never dreamed of. She embraced her new job. When that job closed a few years later, her mother possessed the will and initiative to find an equally rewarding job that she worked for many years and eventually retired from.

Dr. Walker-Green assisted her mother with not only changing her situation but also interrupting the oppressive norm for women at that time. This shifted her mother's thinking, from accepting expectations that conflicted with her natural abilities. No longer did her mother conceal her abilities or succumb to what others thought. She confidently built her skill set for the workforce. In addition, she lessened the probability of poverty because she worked and provided for her children. Dr. Walker-Green and her mother stopped two generational curses in their tracks.

After her mother's success, Dr. Walker-Green went on breaking generational curses, including financial instability. While navigating habits she had witnessed in her family and community, Dr. Walker-Green made missteps but committed to learning why she made certain decisions with money and how she could change that. Ironically, this became the focus of her studies and career.

She went on to earn several degrees in finance and business management. With over eighteen years of experience in the financial services industry, she possesses the ability and passion to place the best interest of her clients above her own. Specializing in retirement, estate planning, investment advisory services, and strategic financial planning, Dr. Walker-Green provides state-of-the-art financial services to hundreds of organizations, families, and individuals. Her expertise has helped clients place themselves at their optimum financial position without compromising their immediate cash needs. Coupled with her unparalleled expertise is a genuine concern for providing superior service, long-term financial security, and ultimate success. There is no wonder why she is known as the financial dynamo.

She has been featured in notable publications such as Black Enterprise Magazine, Forbes, and Senior Market Advisor Magazine. She recently published her first book The Inevitable Rise of the Shero Nation, a book that embraces everything that speaks to women, every aspect of what has touched their lives and shaped their personalities. Dr. Walker-Green says, "[This book] addresses our growth, our outlook, our goals, desires, and dreams to strive for and be the best that we can be."

For the accomplished Dr. Walker-Green, it's not about always having it together and keeping it together. It's more about accepting God's grace and assistance to make the right choices and putting proper things into place so that you can live a blessed, undefeated life and also be a blessing to others.

The good news is that anyone, including you, has the power to break generational curses. But first, you must be able to identify what they are and how they affect your family. To identify the generational curses in your family, you must know your family history. Ask questions of family members, not in an intrusive way. But inquire about the who, what, and possible whys to understand key people or events.   Look for patterns that contribute to a defeatist mindset. Search for things like poverty, racism, diseases, teen pregnancies, abusive drug use, alcoholism, obesity, etc. These are all by-products of curses. Understanding them is the first step to breaking them.

Remembering God's Plan
Let me be clear: God is a good God, but he is a God of order. He has set certain universal laws in place that cannot be reversed. He gives us free will to choose our own way with the hope that we will choose Him because He wants us to experience the good plan that He had for us before Adam and Eve's fall in the garden. We have the choice to continually violate those laws and reap the consequences of our sins. Sin is a choice. God wants to bless and prosper you, but if He can't chasten you when you go in the wrong direction, He is not your God. Understand that our God is the epitome of all that is good, righteous, and honorable. He is not a respecter of persons; he does not discriminate when He bestows blessings. He is an equal opportunity God, ready to forgive our sins and give us a better life. One where an undefeated mindset can flourish, and we can prosper.

Before the Fall, God's plan for us was to live in a Utopia Society.

If sin had not been introduced into the world, we would have been living in a perfect world. A utopia typically describes an imaginary community or society that possesses highly desirable or nearly perfect qualities for its members. It may also represent an intentional community, a promised land of sorts.

According to Merriam-Webster, promised land is defined as "something and especially a place or condition believed to promise final satisfaction or realization of hopes." I define it as a place where someone expects to find great happiness. Do you want to find happiness? It's still available. Don't wait forty years for it.

God initially delivered the Israelites from Egypt with the intention of them reaching their destination in eleven days. He had Moses send out twelve spies, and they all came back with a negative report except two, Joshua and Caleb. This contagious negativity led to a prevailing defeatist attitude amongst the tribes, and it cost them another forty years in the wilderness. The entire generation that left Egypt had to be wiped out before the new generation could proceed and possess God's promise.

Always remember that God's plan for you is a good one. The Israelites were ready to leave Egypt for a new home, a promised land of milk and honey. This was a new season for them, and God wanted them to know how to prosper in this new place in their lives. What new endeavor are you about to embark on? God also has a promised land experience for you! In this place, you get a little slice of Heaven here on earth. But like the Israelites, you too must assume the appropriate position to receive God's blessings. Scripture states, "Carefully obey the Lord your God, and faithfully follow all his commands that I'm giving you today. If you do, the Lord your God will place you high above all the other nations in the world" (Deuteronomy 28: 1 NIV). It goes on to list specific blessings.

In essence, God is saying He will bless you, everything you love, and everything that concerns you. You are fearfully and wonderfully made. As a descendant of Abraham, He will bless you everywhere you go and everything you do. He calls you an overcomer, more than a conqueror, blessed and highly favored of the Lord. He will bless you amid turmoil, trials, and tribulations. He calls you victorious before the battle begins. You, mighty woman and man of valor – He calls you undefeated! This is what you will receive if you accept Him as your one and only God! He places His name on you and stamps you with His approval.

When you don't act like you are chosen by God, you deny your spiritual inheritance. In order to wear the victor's crown, you must have an undefeated mentality. To be defeated is a disqualifier. You take your destiny out of the hands of God and become your own judge. Denying the mercy and grace of God makes you a target for Satan.

Scripture is very clear on what happens if you choose not to follow God and His commandments. It states, *"However if you do not obey the Lord your God and do not carefully follow all his commands and decrees I am giving you today, all these curses will come on you and overtake you"* (Deuteronomy 28:15–68 NLT). The curses are the results of choosing to live a defeatist lifestyle.

Generational Blessings
The good news is that you can break the curse by simply repenting and being willing to follow God and be obedient to his word. It's a daily choice to be generational curse breakers. God says, *"When all these blessings and curses I have set before you come on you and you take them to heart wherever the Lord your God disperses you among the nations, and when you and your children return to the Lord your God and obey him with all your heart and with all your soul according to everything I command you today, then the Lord your God will restore your fortunes and have compassion on you*

and gather you again from all the nations where he scattered you"
(Deuteronomy 30: 1–3 NIV). Wow…what a benefits package! This
is what we get to pass on to our children because of our obedience.

Even when we miss the mark, God is still faithful. He ever so
patiently waits on us to embrace the blessings that He provides for
us in His covenant. Scripture reminds us that "The Lord is not slow
in keeping His promise, as some understand slowness. *Instead, He
is patient with you, not wanting anyone to perish, but everyone to
come to repentance"* (2 Peter 3:9 NIV). No one is disqualified from
having access to all that God has in store for those who choose to
live an undefeated life.

CHAPTER FIVE
A Defeatist Mindset – When Fear Is Your Master

"What if it gets me when you turn off the lights?" "The monster. He might be hiding in my closet." "I am so scared." As improbable as they seem, these are genuine words of an innocent child who will eventually learn that our imaginations can sometimes get the best of us.

That is why Scripture encourages us to *"[cast] down imaginations, and every high thing that exalteth itself against the knowledge of God..."* (2 Corinthians 10:5 KJV). We should always assess our thoughts, especially if they don't align with what we know according to the Word.

Did you notice the child's hypothetical words? I point those out because *could bes* and *would bes* often hijack adult thoughts. Sometimes we are so busy thinking about the *what-ifs* and things that *might* happen that we miss out on the real journey (where they never occur). If we don't manage our wandering thoughts, they will spiral out of control and put us on a rabid track riddled with unwarranted fear. When those childhood monsters transform into adult issues we *could* face or a circumstance that *might* blow up, we must find a way to navigate those thoughts. Better yet, we must actively debunk and deny them because they are not from God.

The Master of Fear
At the root of all sin is fear. Fear is commonly referred to as **F**alse **E**vidence **A**ppearing **R**eal. False meaning that what you see or think isn't based on truth. So if it's false, it's false! Evidence is whatever supports this untruth: accusations, lies, assumptions, or manipulative actions. Appearing is the falsehood that hides the lie or cover-up. Real is the actual truth that is contrary to what is being portrayed.

The master of fear is Satan. We know this because God is love. And *"perfect love casts out fear"* (1 John 4:18 ESV). That leaves Satan as the source of fear.

We also know that Satan is our enemy and forever adversary. He doesn't hide this either. In fact, he boldly stands as "an accuser of brethren," which means he points the finger of false blame at God's children every chance he gets. But his schemes reach far beyond fabricated accusations. I am not sure why I've chosen "glossy" words to describe Satan and what he stands for. But here it is: Satan is a straight-up liar! He always has been and always will be.

You might wonder what his lies have to do with our fear. Lies and fear seem unrelated, but therein lies his masterful skill of leveraging the two for his selfish benefit. To truly understand his cunning nature, we must think about why he does what he does. How does it help him to make such accusations against us?

It's simple. He wants to "weaken our influence and injure our cause for which we have been identified."[27] He wants to make us look like bad representatives as children of God. His main job is to sabotage you to the point of either ineffectiveness or nonexistence. You are that much of a threat to his kingdom. His tactics aren't new, but he's used them for a long time. He continuously uses the same pranks because they work.

Fear is at the top of his list for immobilizing Christians. It breeds lies, deceit, and deception. He sets the stage for an academy award performance by creating an illusion and sprinkling elements of truth here and there for validity. Or he may offer to give you something you've always desired, but for a price that will ultimately cost you your soul.

Regarding fear, he starts small, with lies that confirm our fears, insecurities, and weaknesses. He searches for our most vulnerable thoughts. Then he continuously manipulates them until he can breach and invade our minds. From this point, the real attack begins.

[27] King James Bible Dictionary. (n.d.). Retrieved July 20, 2022, from https://kingjamesbibledictionary.com/Dictionary.

Remember how it all started with the monster? It began with "what if" the monster does this. Those thoughts quickly progressed to the monster eating the child by the end. Do you see how those upgraded thoughts lead to something we fear the most? They put us in a state of mental torture.

From an adult standpoint, he uses individuals with lying lips or people who are also hurting and fearful to build a fire underneath us to intensify the hold that fear has on us. He doesn't stop there.

He creates situations that support his lying premise and confirms that what we feel is the truth. Then hopelessness, condemnation, and shame show up to render us completely useless to God. The lens that we see life through is corrupted to the point where everything that we see, do, or think is influenced by it. We become so fearful that we are paralyzed to the point of isolation. Then Satan comes in to finish the job. His ultimate goal is total annihilation. His aim is suicide or death. You are a threat to his kingdom because you've chosen God. If he can't kill you, he will immobilize you and render you fruitless.

Conquering Fear

We aren't equipped to fight Satan; where we fall short is in our humanity. Remember Eve's actions in the Garden of Eden? She was deceived into thinking that she could befriend the snake and walk away like a goddess with the gift of knowledge that her new confidante had bestowed upon her. Basically, Eve thought that she could have her cake and eat it too, but it cost Eve her rightful place in God's kingdom. She lost the opportunity to reap the benefits listed in Deuteronomy[28]; through serving God with all her heart and being the apple of His eye. According to Scripture, *"The thief [Satan] comes only to steal and kill and destroy; I [Jesus] have come that they may have life, and have it to the full"* (John 10:10 ESV). Our only hope, our only salvation is in Jesus.

To live a life undefeated we must examine the life of Jesus and follow His example.

First, we must examine ourselves by doing a checkup from the neck up. What's actually going on in our minds? God says, *"Finally, brothers and sisters, whatever is true, whatever is noble, whatever is right, whatever is pure, whatever is lovely, whatever is admirable – if anything is excellent or praiseworthy – think about such things"* (Philippians 4:8 NIV). We must question every thought and even question our answers. Even if it's something that someone else said, how we perceive it is ultimately how we (individually) experience it or live it out loud. So honesty with self is critical to renewing our minds and preparing for living an undefeated lifestyle.

Dr. Brenè Brown, a researcher specializing in social work, says this about fear, "People buy into [fear] and feel fear because they don't have the language to attach to what it is..."[29] When you can define fear, specifically your fear, you can become a giant killer like David.

We all have our Goliaths. Many times, our giants are lies we create and believe about ourselves. Begin by asking every thought if it is true. Stop creating your own giants, obstacles, and roadblocks with false inner accusations and by creating false evidence. Sometimes you can be your biggest enemy. Don't allow Satan the opportunity to use you to dismantle your purpose.

Sometimes we may be afraid to move forward because of a fear of failure. Find the strength and courage that Joshua found to lead the Israelites into their promised land after the death of Moses. God told Joshua that He was with him, and God encouraged him to be strong and courageous. I believe that God would not have told Joshua to do so if it were not possible. Remember, God is not

---

[28] Total History. (2013, September 25). Deuteronomy chapter 28 summary. Retrieved July 28, 2022, from https://totallyhistory.com.
[29] Podrazik, J. (2013, April 8). Watch: The surprising ways you express fear without realizing it." *HuffPost*. Retrieved September 5, 2022, from https://www.huffpost.com.

a respecter of persons. You too possess the power to move forward. You will not be held back by the lies of the enemy. You are able because you have an undefeated mindset.

Brenè Brown reminds us of President Theodore Roosevelt's words, which relate to having a more than a conquerer mindset in the midst of having a fear of failure:

> It is not the critic who counts; not the man who points out how the strong man stumbles, or where the doer of deeds could have done them better. The credit belongs to the man who is actually in the arena, whose face is marred by dust and sweat and blood; who strives valiantly; who errs, who comes short again and again, because there is no effort without error and shortcoming; but who does actually strive to do the deeds; who knows great enthusiasms, the great devotions; who spends himself in a worthy cause; who at the best knows, in the end, the triumph of high achievement, and who at the worst, if he fails, at least fails while daring greatly, so that his place shall never be with those cold and timid souls who neither know victory nor defeat.[30]

Remember, Satan is the biggest accuser (critic) of the brethren. He may cause others to judge you and condemn your good reputation. Rather than standing in angst or fear about what people may think of you, hold your head up with godly confidence knowing that in Him you live, move, and have your being (Acts 17:28). You have access to God's grace and mercy as well as the Holy Ghost power within to fuel your thinking and actions for the Kingdom.

That alone should be the foundation of your combative, undefeated stance with a laser-focused goal to defeat the enemy. An undefeated mindset is stronger than judgment. It will completely wipe out self-judgment and the fear of the judgment of others. It's dangerous to consider what other people say about you because it has the power to negatively influence how you think about yourself.

[30] Roosevelt, T. The man in the arena. *TR Center*. (n.d.). Retrieved September 5, 2022, from https://www.theodorerooseveltcenter.org.

Scripture tells us that we should bring every captive thought *"to the obedience of Christ"* (2 Corinthians 10:5 KJV). So after pulling those destructive illusions from the high places in our minds, we must then line them up with the Word of God. This is where they belong because it encourages us to think about what God has to say about the matter. God wants you to think about your thinking. Challenge your harmful thoughts. Then convert them into God's given truth. This specifically means God gives you the power to take control of your feelings and think empowering undefeated thoughts.

When we know what God thinks of us and trust Him, we are safe. God has assured us that *"...no weapon formed against us shall prosper"* (Isaiah 54:17 KJV). The enemy forms footholds in our minds that grow into strongholds. In other words, he sees an open door, puts his foot in it to open it completely, and then he comes in and builds a fortress of wrong thinking in our minds. A stronghold is a place that has been fortified to protect itself against attack. It's a place where a particular cause or belief is strongly defended or upheld. The enemy is well aware of our humanity. He appeals to our carnality. Carnality pertains to pleasures of the flesh or body. It seeks to fulfill desires, passions, and appetites. It is not spiritual; rather, it is simply human and worldly. Most people that slip into carnality don't recognize how or when they got there. The process can be subtle and gradual, and it can easily happen to the most seasoned and secure Christian. You don't usually go from being spiritually minded to carnally minded in one moment or instance. It happens in a series of events. Here are some examples:

- King David was a lover of God. He was beloved of God and characterized as a friend of God. Yet, he was also a master manipulator and murderer. Over time, David worked through his carnality. He sought God's instruction. Ultimately, through prayer, God redeemed his life, and He was completely restored to undefeated status.

- The Apostle Paul had one assignment, he was on a mission to kill Christians. He had a life-changing experience on the road to Damascus. He went from murderer to becoming an apostle, and ultimately he wrote more books in the Bible than all the other disciples. Paul received a total life transformation. He did not stay the person that he had become. He laid down defeated thinking and picked up a new mantle, an undefeated mindset.

Remember Satan is not your friend. He proved that to Eve in the Garden of Eden. To counteract his plan, you must demolish all walls and fences that have been built to defeat you. You can only do this in the power of the Holy Spirit whom Jesus sent to help you here on earth. You are undefeated because it's a fixed fight. The intent of the serpent in the garden was to derail the plan of God for your life with fear, but God is always one step ahead of Satan. Whether the battle is external or internal, God has given you the tools to conquer fear and win!

FEAR: AN INDICATOR, NOT A NAVIGATOR
I've talked a lot about the negative side effects of fear. In a way, I am grateful for fear – not the spirit of fear, but the emotion of fear. It is through fear that we ask questions that only faith can answer. Fear indicates concerns. After reflecting on concerns that may need to be addressed, we can activate our faith.

As long as we understand that fear should only evoke questions, and; it does not provide the answers, we are more apt to use it to our benefit. If we're stuck on any one question or the other, then we have not allowed ourselves to discover the truths that only faith can bring about. Faith is the answer to the questions that fear arouses. Faith can only come by exposure to the Word of God. In the presence of fear, we should ask questions, then immediately go to the Bible and find the answers. Doing so will silence the questions of fear. Once we have biblical-based answers, those questions will no longer haunt our minds or spirits.

By doing this our anxiety decreases and becomes easier to handle, and we can move forward in faith, period. If you are a fearful person, that means that you have a lot of concerns, and you need to address those concerns before you move forward. You shouldn't do that just by talking to people. Please don't misunderstand me. You should utilize the community of people God placed around you. Communicating your concerns to them is part of using relationships with the people God blessed you with. However, avoid relying on people alone. Take your concerns to God because He gave you the emotion of fear as an indicator that something that needs to be done before moving forward. We move forward cautiously, but we continue to move forward. We don't allow fear to paralyze or stop us; we use it as a warning to proceed with caution. In this way, fear is an indicator, not a navigator.

Joan Montreuil is a great example of someone who used fear as an indicator rather than a navigator. She mastered her fear and used it to overcome adversity. At certain times in her life, fear of the unknown could have gained control and affected some of her pivotal life decisions. She broke that cycle as you'll see by all that she has accomplished.

When she was seventeen and midway through her senior year of school, she learned that she was pregnant with her first child. Montreuil soon found out that her child's father wanted nothing to do with her. He broke promises of support and commitment to Montreuil, the person he once referred to as his "one and only." She was devastated, but not as much as those who loved her and had great big dreams for her life. Everyone turned their backs on her, including lifelong friends, relatives, and mentors. The thing that grieved Montreuil the most wasn't the fact that she had to grow up overnight, but that she'd broken her mother's heart into a million pieces.

Fearful of how her life would unfold, Joan struggled with depression and was confused about how to move forward. She thought of herself as the next teen statistic that everyone wanted to avoid. She says, "I was too depressed to seek GOD, too far out to hear Him, and too embarrassed to repent." Alone and afraid, Montreuil was on the verge of allowing fear to chart the course of her life. Disoriented by everything taking place, Montreuil even forgot one of the most important lessons her grandmother had taught her: Learn to communicate with God. Seek after Him, His grace, and His wisdom.

God remembered His child. According to Montreuil, God loved her enough "to awaken [her] spirit and saved [her] life and the life of [her] unborn child." She shares exactly how God did it:

> In all of my misery, I heard this song on the radio called "I'm Walking on Sunshine." I had never heard this song before, but it brought light to my soul in a dark period of my life. Now I've heard many songs, but this one had a profound impact. Being that I was a black teen, depressed and lost, the odds of becoming interested in a pop song sung by a country artist was second to none in my book. But GOD will take the foolish things to confound the wise! (1 Corinthians 1:27 NIV). I was mentally exhausted, and he used a secular song to bring me out. God had given me a song that would not remain silent; it became my theme song during the course of my pregnancy. This was the boost that I needed to go on and give life to this child that GOD had allowed me to conceive.

That was only the beginning of what God would do in Montreuil's life. God broke the grip of fear and lifted Montreuil high above her circumstances and strengthened her for the journey. He gave her the heart of an undefeated champion.

Today, Montreuil is a proud mother of six and has been happily married to her supportive husband, Byron, for 37 years. She is also a seasoned author of three self-help books, *The Unexpected, Delivered From Destruction, and Beyond The Vows*. She's been awarded several times by the Screen Actors Guild for her work in film and television. In addition, she has been a guest on countless talk shows, featured in several articles, and contracted celebrity appearances. Montreuil is known as a literary guru! She writes, directs, produces, and edits her own films by choice!

Through her determination, she has overcome many challenges that made her the strong woman she is today. As a result of her experiences, Joan always sought to be a servant leader. She is an ordained minister and puts her money where her mouth is. In 1993 Joan founded and formed a group Sister II Sister along with her sister Wanda Bryant. This sisterhood association consisted of writers, singers, and actors who would travel throughout New Orleans' impoverished neighborhoods performing stage plays and spreading the message of faith and love. For Montreuil, this is a labor of love. Although it came with many challenges, she would not trade it for anything. Throughout her journey, she has met some incredible women who share similar visions for women in film. They have come together under her leadership and formed an all-female writer's team and production crew.

Not bad for a teen mom whom everyone thought was doomed to fail in life, right? With God's help and a song, the cage of fear was broken. Once it no longer guided her, that little spark grew into the determination and unstoppable drive that made Montreuil so successful. That drive is what makes her a true example of an undefeated champion.

God graciously takes those who willingly go into new seasons, placing them in new destinations. He never ceases to do exceedingly, abundantly, and above all we could ever ask or think (Ephesians 3:20). He's been blowing the minds of many for thousands of years. Remember God has marvelous things in store for you.

CHAPTER SIX
You Are Undefeated

I've heard that "a mind is a terrible thing to waste."[31] This statement certainly applies to this discussion, especially when you think about your life of purpose and all that God has called you to be. You were given your mind as a tool to glorify God. Your brain is the control center of your entire body; it influences everything about you. That's why assuming your rightful position as a child of God with an undefeated mindset is so important.

We've been talking about an undefeated mindset throughout this book, I'd be remiss if I did not include a discussion about the building blocks of the mind. Discussing psychology and the way the human mind works is a complex thing. I know because I studied it during my undergraduate. Through my studies, I have learned and come to understand what man proclaims as scientific proof. But how many of you know that our knowledge is likely minuscule compared to our Creator's mastery of this topic? I must admit my explanation may come nowhere near our Creator's definition for it. His thoughts are way higher than mine. With that said, here is my understanding of the brain and mind.

Brain vs. Mind
Merriam-Webster defines the mind as, "the part of a person that thinks, reasons, feels, understands, and remembers." In the APA Dictionary of Psychology, psychologists define the mind as a place where "all intellectual and psychological phenomena of an organism [happens], encompassing motivational, affective, behavioral, perceptual, and cognitive systems..."

So, is the mind the same thing as the brain? It depends on whom you ask. There are two basic schools of thought. When talking about one or the other, some use mind and brain interchangeably. They think the two are one and the same. Others think the mind is the mental part of the brain, and the actual brain itself is the physical part. The mind can't be physically touched, but the brain

[31] In 1972 the United Negro College Fund used the slogan, to support its efforts to promote the necessity of education.

can. I am not here to refute any one claim or confirm another. Rather, my discussion simply relates to how our thought processes directly impact the mindset that we have.

The Brain

To explain how complicated the brain is and its interconnectivity with other parts of our body would take more time and pages than we have for this book. According to John Hopkins Medicine, "the brain sends and receives chemical and electrical signals throughout the body. Different signals control different processes, and your brain interprets each." The brain assumes responsibility for everything related to our movement, how we perceive things, and our mental processes.[32]

The brain has three distinct areas: the prefrontal cortex (lobes), the limbic system, and the brain stem (See Illustration 1). Each area of the brain connects to a specific set of functions. For example, the prefrontal lobes are considered the executive state, which deals with our logic and reasoning. When questions such as "What can I learn from this?" or other related thought processes arise, the executive state has been activated. The limbic system is thought of as the emotional control center, as it generates questions related to feelings such as, "Am I loved?" The brainstem responds to the limbic system to determine an individual's safety. Essentially, the brain makes sense of our experiences and plays a major role in thoughts and perceptions.

The Mind

I am sure we can agree that the mind cannot be touched. It's an abstract place of sorts. A place of unlimited thoughts and ideas. So much flows in and out of the mind, which is why it should be carefully managed. Undeniable power resides there.

---

[32] Brain anatomy and how the brain works. Johns Hopkins Medicine. (2021, July 14). Retrieved July 28, 2022, from https://www.hopkinsmedicine.org.
[33] Spigelmyer, L. (2022, July 22). Children's emotions. The Behavior Hub. Retrieved August 1, 2022, from https://www.thebehaviorhub.com.

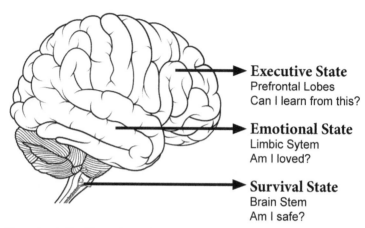

Executive State
Prefrontal Lobes
Can I learn from this?

Emotional State
Limbic Sytem
Am I loved?

Survival State
Brain Stem
Am I safe?

Illustration 1. The Human Brain. (Georgetown University Center for Child and Human Development)[33]

Power to Derail. What happens when you run into a situation that starts with the anticipated logical question (What can I learn from this?), but then your thoughts unexpectedly go awry? For example, you conclude what you can learn from a certain situation but began to wonder if you have what it takes to apply that newfound learning. You might think things like: "Yes, I learned something new, now what? Does my skillset really help me to demonstrate what I learned? Will people I show trust me or even think I know what I am talking about?" Do you see how easily doubt can ignite an inner critic within? This is dangerous because it might derail the path of discovery you were placed on that would lead to other opportunities. If you are not careful, undesirable thoughts will hijack the whole experience and alter your course.

Power to Propel. Our thoughts can also move us forward. Forward movement happens because of the potential within our thoughts. You've probably heard the breakdown of achievement being 10% inspiration and 90% perspiration. Pay close attention to the 10%;

don't sleep on it. Without inspirational thoughts, people who achieved great things would not have known where to focus their efforts. It all starts with what is going on in our minds. The right thoughts will propel us on our purposed path.

We are meant to be vessels for God's work; it's not enough to have a functioning brain with flowing thoughts. God wants us to use our abilities for His glory. He wants us to have a receptive mind and body. It is about far more than the gray matter sitting in our heads. Rather, it is about the level to which our thoughts reduce or elevate – how they derail or propel us.

The ultimate goal is to have thoughts that cultivate an undefeated mindset. And God provides clear instructions that not only guarantee an undefeated mindset but also secure it.

An Undefeated Mind: God's Instructions
We are complex beings created by an amazing God! So, what does He say about the mind? God reveals a lot about the mind in Scripture. We've already discussed some in this book. Here are a few more:

This is the covenant I will establish with the people of Israel after that time, declares the Lord. I will put my laws in their minds and write them on their hearts. I will be their God, and they will be my people. (Hebrews 8:10 NIV)

Have you ever been provided with confusing or unclear instructions? Well, that's something we never have to worry about with God. We don't have to wonder about anything that God wants us to do or how He would have us do it. He writes His expectations upon the hearts of His creation. Our Hearts! When His mind is within us, the mind makes the connection. Of course, the mind of God is undefeated, and we see this reflected in a person who has an undefeated mindset.

Do not conform to the pattern of this world but be transformed by the renewing of your mind. Then you will be able to test and approve what God's will is – his good, pleasing and perfect will. (Romans 12:2 NIV)

Why must we be cautious about "the pattern of the world"? Let's face it; things of the world today are different – and not for the better. For example, top-rated television shows are not what they use to be. Back in the day, shows promoted unity of the family and finding solutions to problems in the world. Now, shows with the highest ratings are all about drama, shock effects, and other suggestive details. The worldly culture continues to decline year after year. That's why we are warned about embracing the negativity that the world bombards us with as truth on a daily basis. This is where scripture memorization comes in. It is the fuel that energizes our renewed minds to perform the will of God.

...for, "Who has known the mind of the Lord so as to instruct him? "But we have the mind of Christ. (1 Corinthians 2:16 ESV)

As finite human beings, our mentality is limited. There is no way we can comprehend what's going on in God's mind because He is the Alpha and Omega of all things. In other words, He is all-knowing. But we can have the mind of Christ and model our behavior according to His biblical example. He shared His thoughts with us throughout the New Testament for that purpose. Look to His example for guidance.

Set your minds on things above, not on earthly things. (Colossians 3:2 KJV)

Things on earth can be all-consuming. Keeping the home running. Taking care of children. Maintaining relationships with our spouse, significant other, family members, or friends. Doing our best on the job. Those things are important, but we can so easily get bogged down in them. Not to mention, other things are competing for our attention like the barrage of emails, texts, voicemails, phone notifications, and social media posts (because we wish we could see all of them). It's not that these things are not important; they have their proper places. When we look at our earthly resources and then look at our godly purpose, it may seem impossible. That's why it's important to adopt the attitude that David had. All things are possible with God!

You will keep him in perfect peace those whose mind is stayed on You because he trusts in You. (Isaiah 26:3 NKJV)

One of God's personalities is Jehovah Shalom. It means Prince of Peace. Some Christians live a life of unnecessary anxiety and worry because they don't seek God daily and dwell in His presence. What a huge loss! We should seek the mind of God. There is so much to learn and know about Him as a person. We have so much to gain if we seek to know Him. He is able to give us peace that surpasses all understanding when we stay focused on Him and His purpose for our lives. This popular saying is true: "Know God, know peace. No God, no peace."

Scripture is the language of God! He speaks to the undefeated spirit that resides in you with wisdom, instruction, and empowerment. His Word never changes. It is all-powerful, and it is life-changing. He created you to hear His voice. Deep down inside of you, the Holy Spirit is waiting for His marching orders. God knew that we would face a crossroads where we would be confronted with the limitations of our humanity. Building an undefeated attitude is important because your attitude determines how high you will go in life.

The 1990's: The Era of the Mind
God promised us an undefeated status in His Word, and He outlines how we can achieve it. However, it took time for us to collectively catch on to it. During the 1990s, however, Christians

began to take a serious look at the power of the mind.

A wave of mind consciousness moved through our community, and we began to have real conversations about the mind and how it affected our Christian walk. In 1994, Joyce Meyer opened up the conversation about the mind, will, and emotions with her popular book, *The Battlefield of the Mind*. Her all-time bestselling book explains how to control the thousands of thoughts we have every day. It also helps us to recognize damaging thoughts that hinder the undefeated mindset. She said, "Our actions are a direct result of our thoughts. If we have a negative mind, we will have a negative life. If, on the other hand, we renew our mind according to God's Word, we will prove 'the good and acceptable and perfect will of God' for our lives."

Two years later, Bishop T.D. Jakes blazed the nation with his book, *Woman Thou Art Loosed*, which led to a book series, an international conference, a play, and a film. Women's minds were shifting away from pain, suffering, failure, and defeat to faith in God and the undefeated lifestyle that God promised. Most people may not be aware that *Woman Thou Art Loosed* was based on a true story. It resonated with the hearts and minds of many and garnered positive reviews from authors and critics alike.

During the 90s, Christian creativity began documenting the everyday problems and harsh experiences of humanity. This evoked real discussions about responding to these experiences. Joyce Meyer and Bishop T.D. Jakes are two of several authors who produced work during this time that deepened our understanding of how we could work the mind to better attend to daily life. They brought about a level of introspection that prompted us to begin thoughtfully considering how to successfully navigate unwarranted and unfortunate situations, thus, bringing about the spirit of the undefeated champion.

Unapologetically Undefeated

At one point, women needed more confidence to recognize why and how they could live undefeated. Fortunately, the 1990s led to more women living unapologetically undefeated. This mindset is necessary, especially for women. It is stronger than judgment, insecurities, shame, guilt, embarrassment, vulnerability, and even mental torment. It promotes self-acceptance and self-worth. It also increases one's personal value.

Native Houstonian and Texas A&M University graduate, Kim Davis knows this first hand. In 1995, she began her journey in a highly-competitive career. Being an aspiring female journalist in a male-dominated field of work meant relentlessly pursuing her goal. She built a successful career in media communications and consulting because she set out with unwavering determination, worked diligently, and maintained an undefeated attitude. "In the sports industry [undefeated] means never losing games," Davis said. "For me though, it just means never quitting."

Davis admits her success didn't come easy, especially in the beginning. She recounts the very first interview she ever went on for an internship:

> When I was in college, I sought out my very first internship at Channel 11. Now, this was a free internship, and I applied in person. I was interviewed by a managing editor. He told me not only could I not have an internship, but also that he thought I should change my major. He also said that I had no future in this industry, and additionally he thought I had some sort of a speech impediment.

As a pastor, I work with many young bright minds who are eager to make a difference in their chosen careers. I cringe when I think about how Davis must have felt after interviewing for a chance at interning. Talk about a blow to an inexperienced person's self-esteem! Davis admits that this experience "would've defeated a lot of people." But it didn't defeat her. She explains how she found a way:

By chance, my sister knew someone who knew Carolyn Campbell. She worked on the consumer hotline for Channel 11, and I had the chance to be an intern under her. I will never forget the day I saw the guy that had previously interviewed me while walking through the building. He asked, "What are you doing here?" I simply responded "Oh yes, I'm an intern. I work on the consumer hotline." I stuck with it and later I was able to obtain an internship in the news and sports department.

Challenges did not stop there for Davis as obtaining experience also came with certain difficulties:

> The way it worked in our industry when I started was like this: You went to a smaller market to gain experience. Smaller market TV stations have only two people in their sports department. Well, the chances of one of those small-town news directors making me one of those two people was slim. Because I had worked at the TV station in College Station-Bryan, Texas (Channel 11), I had a tape when I graduated from Texas A&M. I had what a lot of people coming out of college didn't have on my resume. I had experience, I had references. Yet, I still couldn't find anything. I decided to go and write for newspapers because that would give me credibility as a journalist. At that time, there were really no women or very few in the industry. I began writing for the Houston Sun and doing some freelance work for the *Houston Post.*

Writing for newspapers wasn't her ultimate goal, so she did not get comfortable there. She pursued other options like writing for the wire services to cover the Houston Oilers. She attended their practices as well as traveled to cover the team on the road. In addition, Kim worked a bit in radio. She followed her plan to get experience and build credibility as a journalist. By no means was it easy. She encountered one obstacle after another including racism, sexism, stereotypes, and anything else you could name that came along with being an African-American woman in a male-dominated workforce. Despite all of her challenges, Kim persevered and earned other opportunities.

Kim Davis knew she deserved a place in the sports industry, and the way she showed up had to communicate this. She always dressed and conducted herself as a professional. She prepared for every assignment and followed all of the rules. Davis emphasizes her reason for doing so: "I've fought too hard in my entire career to earn this level of respect and be considered credible."

Today, Davis is the president and chief strategist at The KD Company, a media communications consulting firm helping corporations, institutions, professional service firms, and C-level executives develop a disciplined strategic approach to transformative communication. Even with twenty-seven years of working at various levels in the sports industry (including experience as a news reporter and anchor across four states and being a two-time Emmy award-winning anchor), Davis still has to fight for credentials. She admits that it doesn't seem to get any easier:

> Some days... I don't feel defeated, but I feel a little dejected. Sometimes I sit back and ask myself, "Why do you do this?" I'm sure I could make a ton more money as a communication vice president for some big corporation. Well, I have my own company, and I'm like, "Should I just do that?" And then I'm like, "No, I do this because I feel like my voice is needed." And that's when I say, "I'm not going to be defeated. I'll be done when I decide I'm done, but there's so much work left to do.

Do you see how the situation sometimes gets to her, but she doesn't let it get the best of her? Davis's undefeated journey teaches so much. First of all, as undefeated champions, we must remember that a noteworthy reputation is earned, not given. So, fighting is involved. Fighting to maintain self-worth. Fighting to earn opportunities. Fighting to add value during those earned opportunities. Fighting for respect. And fighting to stand after the respect has been earned. Finally, Davis's journey shows us who has the final say. She never settled or accepted anyone's "no." She maintained what she calls her "driven passion and desire for excellence, not for perfection." Her work "at a level of excellence" coupled with God's grace resulted in her ability to continue on her successful career path as a champion on the field, in business, and life. She is undefeated and unapologetically so.

Restoration of the Mind

Since we've been talking about the mind, this might be a good place to talk about what was going on in my little head during the late 90s. Earlier, I mentioned winning *America's Funniest Videos'* grand prize and global fame for a video showing me screaming my ABCs. The excitement that came with that winning experience was exhilarating. I was far too young and innocent to be affected by the stress of it all. I walked into that situation totally unbothered with childlike faith that I now recognize was an undefeated mindset.

People in our community, school, and church would be so bold as to request a share of our winnings. Reflecting now, I realize that I began losing trust and faith in people at an early age. I started to believe that everyone wanted something from me. That soon erupted into defeat. It was too much for my developing mind to handle. Without telling anyone I contemplated suicide. The thoughts ruminated in my mind. I had intense regret and felt a deep sadness about what I couldn't do for others. I couldn't understand why they were thinking I had something that I didn't. It crushed me. As much as I knew that a bottle of pills would take me out, I was fully aware that I could tell my parents what was going on. But I did not. This is what a defeated mindset will do even in a child. Outwardly, a person may appear undefeated, but inwardly the person may be moving towards madness. I am grateful that I ultimately got my head in a better place with God's help. Without my strong Christian foundation, I would have become a statistic. I had an intensely traumatic experience that could have scarred me for life.

God has called me to help others, true. This was evident early on in my childhood. My empathy for the pain they were feeling because of their perceived poverty put me in a dark place. I had the right idea at the wrong time in my life. Psychiatrist Dr. Alauna Curry concluded that practicing empathy is the cure for psychological trauma.[34] That is exactly what I did. I turned that childlike desire into a mission to equip people to become financially independent. When you know the truth, you are responsible for choosing the freedom that God has given you. The power of the mind and its ability to propel us and its ability to derail us is mind-boggling, pun intended. I now have several undergraduate degrees in psychology and a master's in divinity, all used to equip me to answer God's call on my life the right way.

My lighthouse rescue when I was mentally shipwrecked came in the form of me recognizing the restorative power of God within me. I took the fact that God will never leave me nor forsake me to heart. Because the love of God is greater than our human comprehension, Jesus left us a helper in the form of the Holy Spirit to be our constant companion. The Father, Son, and the Holy Spirit make up a team far greater in power than any formidable force you may face.

When you recognize who's on your team and the power they possess and what God has invested in you, you'll realize you are in an undefeated position. The Bible clearly states, *"You, dear children, are from God and have overcome them, because the one who is in you is greater than the one who is in the world"* (1 John 4:4 NIV). Now it's time for you to assume your rightful position and act like

---

[34] "Trauma." Dr. Alauna, Trauma Psychiatrist. Retrieved July 20, 2022, from https://www.dralauna.com/trauma.

the king or queen God ordained you to be. Having an undefeated mindset is your spiritual inheritance. Accept it. Move forward in the power of the Holy Spirit and conquer the world.

CHAPTER SEVEN
Your Undefeated
Battle Cry

When we first started working on the series that led to this book, I was inspired one Sunday. That morning, I arrived at worship service, my sermon prepared and in tow. I was excited about the message, the word that God had spoken to me. I could hardly wait to deliver such a powerful message that would catapult the Inspiration Church family toward living an undefeated lifestyle.

The service began as it always had, but this particular Sunday, as prepared as I was, service took an unpredictable turn. The Holy Spirit showed up, and as worship filled the room, so did the presence of God. The atmosphere was so charged that I was unable to release myself to begin the sermon. The wave of God's presence drifted throughout the sanctuary, so we adjusted our pace and flowed with it. I thought things would settle after twenty minutes, and we'd be able to proceed to the sermon. However, His presence lingered and lingered. The atmosphere never changed. In fact, it became even more consuming.

Every single individual in the room was experiencing an encounter with God. As I glanced across the room, I could see that while together we were indeed sharing in corporate worship, each person was also having his or her own personal experience with God. All I could do was close my notes, and let God be God in the room and the lives of His people.

As I observed, some people were praying aloud; some were gently swaying back and forth; some were singing; some were speaking in their spiritual tongue. Some were gazing on high. Some appeared to be having conversations with God. Some were overcome with tears. Couples tightly held each other. Some people were simply sitting quietly. I remember that there was just so much to take in. The all-consuming power of God was in our presence, transforming people's troubles – their pain, from defeat to undefeated.

You could see, spiritual walls and barriers falling and weights lifted.

If you ever witness a setting like this one, you will quickly realize in those precious moments that nothing else matters – when it's just you and God.

What was God doing? What were the people experiencing? God was controlling the win, and the people were commanding their battle cries.

Prepare for Battle
Earlier we identified the mind as the primary battlefield of the enemy. Records of wars, battles, and military scrimmages are peppered throughout the history books. You may not have had firsthand experience in physical combat, but you are in the Army of God. There is a time when you will be called forth to become a beacon of faith; a time when you must answer the challenge and fight for what you believe in. This often happens in the midst of great controversy. That's when the very integrity of your undefeated mindset will be tested. You must ask yourself how will you respond. Are you ready for combat? Remember, through God we are victorious; He has provided us with the tools and instruction to be His champions. Will you respond with a Holy Spirit-filled battle cry?

What Is a Battle Cry?
The Britannica Dictionary uses the same definition for battle cry and war cry which is "a shouted word or sound used by fighters in battle to give each other courage or to frighten their enemy." The history of the battle cry started with the Romans. The ancient Roman legions traditionally marched in silence to maintain order in their ranks.[35] Once they encountered the enemy, their troops would send up a bone-chilling cry that was meant to intimidate their enemies. Rick Gregory states, "Battle cries are not necessarily articulate, although they often aim to invoke patriotic or religious sentiment" (pg. 213).[36] Imagine being able to change the tide of war with one single action.

There are many examples in the Bible where specific directions during war involved battle cries. For example, before the battle of Jericho, God gave Joshua specific instructions on how to defeat Israel's enemies. Here is a glimpse of that battle:

(Joshua 6:5 NKJV)
It shall be that when they make a long blast with the ram's horn, and when you hear the sound of the trumpet, all the people shall shout with a great shout; and the wall of the city will fall down flat, and the people will go up every man straight ahead."

(Joshua 6:16 NKJV)
At the seventh time, when the priests blew the trumpets, Joshua said to the people, "Shout! For the Lord has given you the city.

(Joshua 6:20 NKJV)
So the people shouted, and priests blew the trumpets; and when the people heard the sound of the trumpet, the people shouted with a great shout and the wall fell down flat, so that the people went up into the city, every man straight ahead, and they took the city.

God gave specific instructions for the war: after you hear the horn, make your unified battle cry heard; the city's wall will fall, and you will overtake it. They obeyed. His power backed their unity and led them through the battle undefeated.

So far, we've talked about physical battles and their accompanying battle cries. What about the spiritual battle cry? Believe it or not, it serves the same purpose. The spiritual battle cry directs the attention of those fighting towards a threat – be it an individual or situation. Now, I need to clarify here. When I say individual, we must remember who the real enemy is. The person in the form of

---

[35] Andrews, E. (2015, May 21). "8 legendary Battle Cries." History.com. Retrieved July 27, 2022, from https://www.history.com.

[36] Gregory, R. 1620: The Story of Thanksgiving. Dog Ear Publishing, 2014, 213.

flesh and blood who stands in front of you is never the real problem. Remember, those "principalities and rulers in heavenly places" go far beyond the difficult person our eyes see. This emphasizes the need for a laser focus on the said threat. Not in a way that makes the threat a sole focus or builds it up to something more important than our God who guides us in conquering it.

The battle cry is our communication to the heavenly realm that our army is on the move with God as our leading general. As we wrestle against principalities and rulers in the higher realm, we need God's guidance. Our battle cry is communication to God that we need and fully accept His help to fight through it. When you think about the purpose of a battle cry and its significance, you begin to understand that it is meant to be a unifier. It gets individuals in the group focused on a set cause. I encourage you to surround yourself with like-minded peers; there is strength in numbers and power in unity. It is a beautiful thing to see God's people set to a single purpose.

An Undefeated Champion's Battle Cry

The term champion implies that an individual gained victory over a challenging circumstance. This life provides us with more than enough of those types of encounters. And when we have no other choice but to face them, we can do so by enacting a battle cry signaling help from God and His Army for the inevitable victory. That's exactly what another undefeated champion does during what she calls "rough places in life."

Author, podcaster, speaker, and entrepreneur, Misty Phillip is an undefeated champion for Christ on the airways. In addition, Phillip is a wife and mother to three grown sons. She recalls the challenges and triumphs of motherhood to younger children and being married to the love of her life.

Parenting is one of the hardest jobs adults are tasked with because children do not come with manuals. Couple that with an unfortunate accident, Phillip found herself in a battle-like situation. She recalls being in a debilitative, helpless state:

> I broke both of my arms in a bicycling accident. I wasn't wearing a helmet, but I was wearing earbuds. One of the earbuds came out, and I thought it was going to get stuck in the wheel. My phone started to slip out of its case. So, I hit the brakes, and when I did, I flipped my bike. Since I wasn't wearing a helmet, I put my arms out to protect my head, and I shattered both of my arms. The whole recovery took me about a year. For the first several months, I couldn't do anything – nothing at all. I couldn't do anything for myself. I couldn't feed myself. I couldn't dress myself. I couldn't bathe myself. I couldn't brush my teeth or go to the bathroom or anything. It was a very humbling time in my life.

Amid this very trying time, Phillip sought the presence of God. She admitted that she couldn't do very much, but she could pray, so she "prayed a lot." She invited God's presence into her situation through her battle cry. Phillip said, "I talked to God a lot about what I was thinking and feeling, and He showed me so much, like how much He loved and cared for me and that I didn't have to do anything. He loved me just because I was His, and He created me."

God's presence and peace comforted Phillip. She had no doubt He was with her, but the battle escalated:

> We lost our health insurance for our special needs son because everybody was taking care of me, but I was unable to take care of anything. Our son was on a special policy that paid for his school which cost $5,000 a month. My arms were broken, and I couldn't do anything when I realized that his insurance had lapsed. It was COBRA, so there was nothing that we could

do. He was going to have to come home because we couldn't afford to put him in school. I cried out to God. Physically, I couldn't do anything to care for him because my arms were broken. I said, "God, for Your namesake and for Your glory, I need You to intervene."

As the situation intensified, so did Phillip's battle cry. She didn't just pray one time for God's presence and peace during this very difficult time. She knew our faithful and able God was right there in the thick of things with her, so she poured out her heart to Him. Even though He already knew the specifics of what was going on, she named them. She released it. Praying and conversing with God was her armor. This was her way of fighting, and God covered the entire situation. Better yet, He brought about what Phillip called "a miracle" that nobody could have predicted:

> Within a couple of weeks, we found ourselves in an office of a Dallas doctor that my husband heard about on a radio talk show. After one of his infant immunizations, our son had a grand mal seizure, and he continued to seize for a couple of days. The doctors said that he was on the autism spectrum. We knew what we were told just didn't ever feel right, but we could never get a proper diagnosis. After my crying out to God and ending up in this doctor's office, after being misdiagnosed for sixteen years, we got a correct diagnosis for him and began to treat the brain disorder that he had.

Who would have ever known that Phillip's battle cry would activate such a powerful response from God? Who could have ever imagined that when God intervened to fix one issue, He would take care of another? He's got it just like that. According to Phillip, God shows himself so faithful, even amid her most current trials and struggles, when in the natural, it doesn't seem like there is a way to fix things when despair tries to set in. God does above all we could ever ask or think. He shows himself faithful in so many areas of our lives. Phillip witnessed this on more than one occasion.

Phillip and her husband have had to assume an undefeated stance together. During their marriage. When their special needs son was born, Connor, they experienced one issue after another. Connor was in and out of the hospital. It was not only a trial for them as parents but also for their marriage. Phillip says,

> Peter had a coworker who was really into pornography, so Peter started looking at pornography. It was damaging our marriage, and I threatened to leave him. I told his mom that he was looking at pornography and that he was living a deviant lifestyle – one I couldn't be a part of that. He confessed his sin to me, and we went and saw our pastor who married us. Our pastor told us that we had to remove those little pebbles, so they don't build up in our relationship.

God didn't leave Phillip and her husband to wrestle with this. She shares how the Holy Spirit showed up in this situation:

> When I forgave Peter, we had an encounter with the Holy Spirit. It was just this incredible experience with the Holy Spirit where we then had to stand together. I had to learn to trust Peter again. Because he had had this kind of secret lifestyle, Peter had to be accountable to me so that I knew everything that he was doing. Ultimately, that was many years ago, and here we are now about to celebrate 30 years of marriage.
>
> So, there's been many things that could have split us apart. The divorce rate for married couples who have a child with special needs is like 90%. We call our marriage forged in fire because, like in knife making, you heat the steel, you temper it, and then you bang on it. But ultimately you build something very beautiful, but it takes the intensity of the

heat and the banging on it to make the marriage. And that's what we have, our marriage has been forged in fire through all of the sanctifying things that we have been through with one another.

No matter what role she fills or where she may find herself in life, Misty Phillip always depends on God's "steadfast support." We serve a God who is concerned about every aspect of our lives. We are able to live undefeated lives because His unwavering love never ceases, and Misty Phillip is a prime example of that.

Commanding Your Battle Cry

When this book started, it began with a war cry from my heart that you would know the Dunamis (power, potential, or ability) that God invested in you before your were formed in your mother's womb. I feel the need to remind you that God gave each of us a spirit of "power, of love, and of sound mind" (1 Timothy 1:7). The same power spoken of in this verse is the same Dunamis within each one of God's children. That's right; you have an inner-working power that God intentionally placed there. A focus on prayer, the Word of God, and the Holy Spirit is the root and strength of your Dunamis. It can and should be used before, during, or after spiritual warfare.

One army, in particular, was aware of the power behind battle cries but neglected to use them to their advantage. Take the Israelite army, for example. Soldiers in the army made great noises and cried, *"A sword for the Lord and for Gideon!"* (Judges 7:20 ESV) as their battle cry before Goliath came out to taunt them, but they never challenged the giant with godly authority.

The "man after God's heart" understood how to utilize a battle cry to his godly advantage. David was deeply rooted in God through his relationship with Him. Therefore, when he needed Dunamis, it was readily available for him. His inner battle cry rose, and he was empowered to defeat Goliath. Your battle cry turns on a supernatural power switch that enables you to be undefeated – no matter the situation.

You should consider your unique situation when determining whether your battle cry will be one of action or hold. Like armies during physical battles, you may actively attack during your battle cry. Or depending on the situation, you resort to what I think of as an active stillness or a holding position. This can also be coupled with a battle cry.

For example, if your financial circumstance looks grim, you may decide to hold whilst trusting and praying to God. You might opt to go into your prayer closet – just you and God. Your battle cry might include sitting there in silence. You might simply close your eyes and invite God's peaceful presence to quiet the noise of worry and calm your wandering mind with a peace that surpasses understanding. You don't have to speak it, but your mind might softly sing the words, "Holy Spirit, You are welcomed right here, right now." This is the heart of your battle cry. Simply allow your mind to sweetly sing this over and over and over again – until you feel His presence. During His presence, you listen as He provides you with practical steps to help you navigate paying bills that are due and gathering necessities for the household. Sometimes an active stillness should precede God's instructions.

On the other hand, a direct attack on your marriage or family might require swift action. Rather than waiting for the enemy to sink your family, and maintain a firm hold on your spouse or children, you have no other choice but to resort to personal and corporate prayer, seek wise counsel, and engage in much-needed conversations with your spouse, children, or other family members. A severe attack on the family often warrants a roaring battle cry – one in which you interject this affirmation:

BY GOD'S POWER,
I'M UNDEFEATED -
I'M UNDEFEATED
I'M UNDEFEATED
I'M UNDEFEATED
I'M UNDEFEATED
I'M READY
WE'RE READY

God has placed a congregation around you to roar with you. There's also a heavenly host rumbling with you. Use it all.

My point is your spiritual battle cry can take on various forms. It is unique to you. You choose it. Everyone's battle cry does not sound the same. In fact, every battle cry is not audible. Whether it be speaking in tongues, praying out loud, stomping, strengthening others, or simply communicating with God; it is our focus, our superpower. Don't just do it. Command it with godly confidence! Your battle cry enables you to maintain your undefeated status and lay claim to your righteous inheritance. Jesus already paid for it, but sometimes you must fight to possess it!

What can stop you? Nothing when God is with you!

God's Win
While you determine and command your battle cry, what do you think God is up to?

He is winning the battle. No matter how small or uncontrollably large (as our human eyes may perceive the situation), God is always on assignment. He ensures that the fixed fight is in your favor, and the victory is yours. When you feel your back is against the wall, and your enemies surround you, God is there. When your enemies outnumber you, and you hear your impending death, God will not fail.

An undefeated king in 2 Chronicles gained this firsthand experience. King Jehoshaphat found himself in a situation where he would likely be defeated. That is until he enacted his battle cry, prayer. The king led his people in a prayer to God in which the king very honestly acknowledged the losing situation they were in. He told God, *"For we have no power to face this vast army that is attacking us. We do not know what to do, but our eyes are on you."* (2 Chronicles 20:12 NIV)

Do you know what message God sent to that king?
There is so much in King Jehoshaphat's prayer, so I am only going to list a few. As you read the list, find your shouting point.

In the face of that vast army, the messenger of God told Jehoshaphat these things:

- "Do not be afraid or discouraged"
- "The battle is not yours, but God's."
- "Take up your positions;"
- "Stand firm."
- "See the deliverance the Lord will give you ..."
- "Do not be afraid; do not be discouraged."
- "Go out to face them tomorrow, and the Lord will be with you."
  (2 Chronicles 20:15-17 NIV)

Have you shouted yet?
If not think about the fact that Jehoshaphat prayed to Almighty God. (Remember, you are in control of your battle cry). As a result, he and his smaller army won the fight. The king and his people were champions that day. God told them that it was His fight, and He never loses (God is ultimately in control of the winning outcome)! It is God's win. Their victory and salvation were guaranteed when they chose to honor Him by being faithful...by having a reverential fear and respect for His divinity.

As Champions of God, He requires us to support things that are true, noble, right, pure, lovely, admirable, and excellent or praiseworthy… to prioritize those things that glorify Him and His creation. Be fearless and undefeated in your representation...be the embodiment of Christ in mind and body.

It remains my prayer that you realize victories are already being won. Why? Because I have the utmost confidence in God, who is the architect of our souls. The Apostle Paul states, *"… being confident of this, that he who began a good work in you will carry it on to completion until the day of Christ Jesus"* (Philippians 1:6 ERV). I am confident that God, the Master Creator will do a complete work in YOU!

CONCLUSION
The Undefeated Focus Group

Some say "knowledge is power." I say only when it is applied. It's one thing to learn the meaning of undefeated and strategies to live that way. It's another thing to read about individuals who unapologetically live this lifestyle. It is yet another thing to have faith that you can live undefeated. However, it is something altogether more powerful when you apply what you have learned. Think about it: what good is faith without works?

This chapter is designed to get you
more engaged in your undefeated journey.

When we started this book development journey, I conducted a focus group to get to the heart of the undefeated subject matter. We interviewed a small group of young adults, both male and female, between the ages of 30 and 52 and asked the following questions:

1. What does the word "undefeated" mean to you?

2. Who or what best exemplifies that definition in today's culture?

3. What does an undefeated lifestyle look like to you?

4. Have you embraced an undefeated lifestyle? How?

5. Is it possible to live an undefeated lifestyle in today's world?

6. If we lived in a perfect world, how would you go about achieving an undefeated life?

7. Define the word "champion."

8. Are all champions undefeated from your viewpoint? If so, why? If not, why?

I share the results of the questions to give you a better idea of how we gauged the development of the content of this book. Their answers were eye-opening to the team of interviewers, and I hope they will help you better measure your perspective on what living an undefeated life means to you.

As you read the questions and their accompanying answers, feel free to highlight words or phrases that resonate with you. Better yet, gather your own focus group of individuals who also commit to the journey of living an undefeated life. Discuss the questions and answers from the focus group and how they apply to your individual lives.

Question: What does the word "undefeated" mean to you?
Answers:
- "No matter what I encounter, I will overcome it!"
- "The word undefeated to me means never giving up or quitting, no matter the circumstance."
- "Undefeated means to me a continuance of generational wealth and self-awareness of my purpose for being here."
- "Undefeated means to overcome every obstacle; to control the mind in every situation.
- "Undefeated means to not give up, preserver amongst the diverse things that you may face in life.
- "Undefeated means to have challenges in your life and you overcome them no matter what, no excuses."
- "Undefeated means overcoming all losses."

Question: Who or what best exemplifies that definition in today's culture?
Answers:
- "Because I'm faced with challenges to grow me, not to defeat me."
- "I would say, [former President] Obama is a person who no matter what was thrown at him or who tried to make him feel less, he still went after what he wanted. He finished the vision of making history and becoming president."
- "In today's culture depending on the generation to which this question was asked, it would depict how they see generational benefits for future individuals. The "why" is selective. It would depend on what undefeated looks like to them."
- "Who - Barack Obama; he exemplifies the following characteristics: sound mind, overcomer, high achiever, someone to look up to and an example of a successful life."
- "Entrepreneurs, people who have been in trouble with law enforcement and overcome, people from the hood that don't see doctors, lawyers, and judges in their neighborhood and became successful."
- "Jay-Z, overcoming where he came from and adapted to the corporate world."

Question: What does an undefeated lifestyle look like to you?
Answers:
- "A life where my purpose isn't stopped."
- "An undefeated lifestyle looks like a person moving forward no matter their circumstances. They can be going through it, but it doesn't show. They don't wear defeat. They wear what they want their life to be."
- "An undefeated lifestyle is mental, physical, & emotional wealth."
- "An undefeated lifestyle is where you get up over and over again; no matter the situation. You must remain positive, and joyful, to be in control of the mind regardless of circumstances; overcome failures."
- "Someone that has continued to get up every day, despite their circumstances, and continue to move forward."
- "Success, again not making excuses, only solutions."
- "Beating all odds and still winning."

Question: Have you embraced an undefeated lifestyle? How?
Answers:
- "Every day, when my purpose is challenged."
- "Yes, every day. I continue to go after my vision and make it my reality. Also, no matter my circumstances, I continue to push forward until it gets better. My focus is the vision."
- "Yes, I do self-care by equipping myself with knowledge daily."
- "Yes. Definitely experienced failure and disappointment, but never wavered from the ultimate goal which is success in all aspects of life. I have joy; not necessarily happy all the time, in every situation, but definitely remain joyful. I do meditation and I stay grounded."
- "Through experiences, I've learned to float with the river, and not try to hold on to the rocks that can prevent me from moving forward in life."
- "Yes, I don't let anything from my past dictate my future… I stay ready so I don't have to get ready."
- "Yes, I believe nothing can stop me, but me."

Question: Is it possible to live an undefeated lifestyle in today's world?
Answers:
- "Yes, by knowing who you are and your purpose, and keeping the right people in your space."
- "I would say it gets hard and you have to focus on a solution. That's the best thing to focus on. What solution you can give or be, or make and not the problem? Figure out what can be done now."
- "Yes, it is possible to have an undefeated lifestyle in today's society where you include caring for others where they are by not allowing what is going on around you to affect your mindset or thinking."
- "Yes, control the mind."
- "At times, it just depends on the stage of life you're in, your environment, and how you react to these occurrences. Every situation is different, and people will handle them differently."
- "It is possible, I feel like the Internet has only brought more to light. God got us!!! Pray every day."
- "Yes, you can still beat the odds."

Question: If we lived in a perfect world, how would you go about achieving an undefeated life?
Answers:
- "By maintaining."
- "If we lived in a perfect world, I would have all the resources and money to make the visions I have a reality and live happily with my family and loved ones traveling & studying history all over the world."
- "In a perfect world, an undefeated life would be that which I live now, mentally sound, emotionally stable, and emotionally fit. Too much of the same is not a good thing."
- "If you can control the mind, stay grounded, you can overcome and always be undefeated. Stay on a steady pathway toward your goals and give back."
- "Promote peace, unconditional love, wealth equality, wisdom, and an abundance of resources."
- "Everything would be perfect, no worries… I wouldn't change anything I've personally been through, it made me who I am."
- "Just working hard and staying focused. Traveling the world."

Question: How would you define the word "champion"?
Answers:

- "Someone who overcame the challenges that challenged their purpose."
- "The word 'champion' is a person who wins and keeps studying what it takes to win and be the best."
- "A champion is a winner at self-awareness."
- "A person who personifies positivity, gives back, and is successful in their own right. They achieve their goals."
- "A resilient person who wins and doesn't give up the first time, but understands the value of getting to the finish line."
- "Someone who overcomes all adversity to become great. Chances make champs!!!"
- "Defeating all odds and winning at this thing called life."

Question: Are all champions undefeated from your viewpoint? If so, why? If not, why?
Answers:

- "Yes."
- "All champions are undefeated in my viewpoint. Because they never give up, no matter what."
- "Not all champions are undefeated. When life hands distractions to individuals, if they are not well equipped in life, this can become self-destructive and they can develop a defeated mentality."
- "Champions are undefeated."
- "Yes. They've proven they can withstand trials and tribulations and pull other people up with them."
- "A champion is undefeated mentally. A true champion must face adversity and overcome it."
- "No. They just haven't met their match."

One of the most powerful revelations that we gained from this experience is the passion and hope that the group had for life. Participants were picked based on age and nothing else. Remarkably, there was a wide range of life experiences in the group. There was a successful realtor, a media entrepreneur, a member of the military, a former gang member turned videographer, an ex-convict turned producer, an accountant, and a mental health counselor.

Just as you live your individual lives, each person in the interviewed focus group had his or her own story to tell. I am honored by their contribution to the success of this book. I am equally grateful that you took the time to read this book and pray that you apply God's truths. I wish every one of them and you an undefeated future full of the grace and love of God.

ABOUT THE AUTHOR

Carlos Jones II is a Houston Texas Native. He was a scholarship athlete at Tennessee State University in Nashville, TN, where he was inducted into the National Football Foundation & College Hall of Fame. He graduated with a B.S. in Psychology. Upon completion of his Bachelors, he went on to complete his Masters in Divinity at Candler School of Theology at Emory University in Atlanta, Georgia. Carlos then went on to serve as a college pastor then executive pastor before stepping into His senior pastor role at Inspiration Church.

He is the author of his first book "Screw It": A guide to successful marriage and relationships, which has traveled the globe.

He is the founder of SCSCC Enterprise, Luxury Car rentals and E-Commerce Automation. He is a mentor to business owners to help them launch and grow and develop their uniqueness.

Carlos Jones is the founding Pastor of Inspiration Church under the covering of Bishop Smokie Norful and the REACH organization. He has incited great growth and leadership. His ministry penetrates the walls of the church as he is also the CEO of Inspiration Partners; a non-profit that is geared towards providing mentoring, life-skill coaching, and exposure to cultural experiences both in and out of our own communities. Carlos is passionate about solutions that heal social injustices, feeds the hungry, and mentors people.

He is an advisor to the board of directors of Southwest Glen Mission and serves on the Houston area Pastors Council, the Fort Bend Pastors council, and is an advisor to Man To Man a non profit catered toward helping men take the next step in life. He is a teacher, director, husband of Sparkle Jones, father of Carlos III and Summer, pastor, adviser and son of Carlos and Stephanie.

A fun fact about Carlos is at the age of 5 he was the first African

American to be the winner and grand prize of $10,000 and $100,000 from Americas funniest Home Videos for doing his ABC's. He was formerly known as the ABC kid!

For more information go to www.carlosjones2.com.

IF YOU LIKED "UNDEFEATED," YOU
WILL LOVE "SCREW IT!"

IT CAN BE FOUND AT ANY BOOK
SELLER RETAIL OUTLET

GET YOUR COPY TODAY!!!

CPSIA information can be obtained
at www.ICGtesting.com
Printed in the USA
BVHW060212011122
650611BV00003B/8